Genuine People

Living & Relating as Real Christians

Stuart Briscoe

Harold Shaw Publishers
Wheaton, Illinois

Library of Congress Cataloging-in-Publication Data

Briscoe, D. Stuart.
Genuine people : living and relating as real Christians / Stuart Briscoe.
   p. cm.
ISBN 0-87788-844-2
1. Christian life. I. Title.
BV4501.2.B734 1995
248.4—dc20   94-44753
                                     CIP

02   01   00   99   98   97   96   95

10   9   8   7   6   5   4   3   2   1

Contents

Contents

Introduction

When the apostle Paul preached, it was not too difficult to measure reactions. Eutychus fell asleep and nosedived from his seat in the window to the floor below with such a crash that Paul had to interrupt his train of thought to attend to him before returning to his final point and the Benediction. In Lystra nobody fell asleep—they were too excited. In fact, they were so excited that they wanted to deify Paul and Barnabas and make sacrifices to them. They didn't fall asleep in Ephesus either. The whole city responded to him—by rioting!

The reactions to my preaching have been much less dramatic. But one Father's Day, years ago, I preached a message entitled "What Do Real Men Eat?" (harking back to the book popular at that time, *Real Men Don't Eat Quiche*). To say it started a riot would be going too far, but it did get the attention of a number of men who habitually suffer from Eutychus syndrome. They surrounded me at the end of the service and said, "You sure gave it to us today. How about doing the same thing to women next week?" So, the next week I preached on "The Real Woman's Issue—Mystique or Mistake?" (borrowing that clever title from *The Feminine Mystique*). We got close to a riot on that one! A man rushed to the front of the church demanding "equal time"!

But the women said, "Our problem is with the men we live with. Do something about marriages." And so it went on for a number of weeks. At least I had no doubt that I was being relevant! And everybody was listening. Eventually it became clear that something so popular in sermon form might also be helpful written down; hence this book. I trust it will keep you awake; but please don't garland me or stone me. Just work through these issues with me with open mind and open Bible.

Although some years have passed since the original version, the questions asked by Christians have not changed. What does it mean to be a real Christian in a world that has so skewed the meanings of manhood and womanhood, parenthood and childhood, marriage, vocation, and ministry? Thank God that his Word is constant even while culture spins in first one extreme direction and then another. The truth remains that Christians find meaning in the time-tested principles set forth in the Bible. It also remains true that the most effective and fulfilled Christians are *genuine*—willing to see life as it is and live life with courage and commitment to the values that make it worth living.

Stuart Briscoe

1

The Meaning of Manhood

Charles Haddon Spurgeon once said, "A Christian is the gentlest of men; but then, he is a man." That's a lofty-sounding sentence. But to make sense of it, we must answer the question "What is a real man?" And what better place to look for the answer than among people who received accolades from Jesus. For as far as he was concerned, John the Baptist was "the greatest": "I tell you, among those born of women there is no one greater than John" (Luke 7:28).

We will first consider how society measures a man, followed by a more detailed study of how Jesus measures him.

Society's Measure of a Man

In our society some confusion continues as to what constitutes a real man. Some years ago, *The 49 Percent Majority: The Male Sex Role* was published. The title refers to the fact that although men comprise approximately 49 percent of the population, they seem to be clearly in the majority because ours is a male-dominated society. The authors, Deborah S. David and Robert Brannon, point out four themes that seem to define the common conception of masculinity. Let's consider these "measures of a man."

No sissy stuff

If you are going to be a real man, you don't eat feminine food or do feminine things like needlepoint (unless you are Rosey Grier, and you can make an exception for him because he's big enough to do anything he likes). A real man doesn't indulge in female talk or enjoy female things. Many sociologists think this is related to a latent fear of homosexuality. So the real man is perceived as a male who never indulges in any kind of sissy stuff.

The big-wheel syndrome

The second identified characteristic of the real man is his need to be in control. Refusing help of any kind, he rejects and ignores the counsel of others. He views himself as clearly a success, and the evidence is on every hand. This man expects everybody to recognize him as the big wheel.

The sturdy-oak syndrome

This third characteristic is closely related to the big-wheel syndrome. It requires the man at all times to be tough, confident, self-reliant, and able to stand firm. He allows everyone else to lean on him because he is the one who will not, under any circumstances, be shaken.

The "give 'em hell" syndrome

The fourth characteristic is colorfully described as the "give 'em hell" syndrome. (I apologize for the language.) This means a real man must be aggressive, daring, and even violent at times. He is highly competitive and makes things happen.

So, if we want to describe what our society considers a real man, we probably would come to the same conclusion as David and Brannon did in their book. However, there is a problem with all of this. When we look at all these big wheels and sturdy oaks, we are forced to recognize that men still die at a younger age than women. They commit 90 percent of all major crime and are responsible for 99.9 percent of all rape and 95 percent of all burglaries. Ninety-four percent of all drunk drivers are men. They also commit 70 percent of all suicides and 91 percent of all offenses against the family.

What can we conclude from this? Evidently, men aren't as in control as we have been led to believe. Things are not going well with these "real men." I wonder why?

Granted, there have been some changes in the last decade and a half. During the 80s men, sometimes in direct response to the outspoken criticisms of women in general and feminists in particular, did make attempts to get in touch with their "feminine side," while in the 90s Iron John led some men into the woods to beat their chests and their drums in an effort to discover their true manhood. Even more recently, the remarkable phenomenon of Promise Keepers has shown that many modern men are looking for a deeper meaning to masculinity in the area of relationships. Time will tell how deeply the male psyche is being touched and changed, but of one thing we can be certain: Change in the right direction, which we will get to shortly, is long overdue.

Jesus' Measure of a Man

Society's definition of a real man is erroneous, and its requirements of him are so burdensome that he really finds it difficult to be a man. He knows inwardly that he isn't able to cope with these heavy demands. For that reason it's time to reevaluate the question "What is a real man?"

The answer comes loud and clear from Jesus. "Hey! If you want to see a real man, take a look at John the Baptist. Because, of all the men born of women, there's never been a greater one than John." John had six characteristics that qualified him as a real man: sincerity, simplicity, conviction, courage, vision, and vulnerability. Let's look more closely at these admirable traits.

Sincerity

John's sincerity was affirmed by the crowds that came to hear him preach. When he spoke, people listened. They found his words so important that they dropped what they were doing and went to hear him. They were attracted by the ring of truth and sincerity in him.

King Herod, who was eventually responsible for John's death, sent for the Baptist even after he was imprisoned. He loved to listen to John. And, even though he wasn't very good at following John's teachings, he was utterly intrigued by the man himself. Why? Because Herod recognized in John a real man of integrity.

John's disciples also testified to his sincerity. Even though the Baptist, at the time of his imprisonment, encouraged some of his disciples to leave him and follow Jesus, we know that they still visited John at regular intervals. They continued to identify with him—they stuck with him and were interested in and concerned about him. Why? Because of his sincerity that had shown through so clearly.

Simplicity

We recognize John's simplicity by his disciplined lifestyle. He ate locusts and wild honey, and wore a garment of camel's hair with a rope around his waist. And he lived in the wilderness. I'm not suggesting you have to do that to be a real man. But I am saying that John was disciplined. He was a man of prayer; he was a man of fasting; he was a man of simple tastes. And like Jesus, he wasn't concerned about fine clothes and the luxuries of life. His simple approach to life was exhibited by a disciplined lifestyle—something worth heeding in these days of affluence and waste.

The simplicity of John's life was also reflected by the directness of his message. He proclaimed that the kingdom of God was at hand and warned people not to waste their time on anything else until they had prepared for it. Don't you like simple, direct people—people who cut through all the frills and froth and get down to the real issues? The world needs men who will say, "Listen, you people, shape up! The kingdom of God is at hand!"

The simplicity of John's message is further illustrated by the way he presented Jesus as the king of the kingdom. He came straight to the point: "There is one coming after me who is preferred before me, the one to whom we look. I'm not the important one. It is he who is all important." He understood the supreme importance of the kingdom, and was unequivocal about the greatness of the King. He presented his truth to the people and called them to repentance, confession, and commitment. Converted people were expected to demonstrate the change in their lives by a completely different attitude toward God and life itself. This is simple, straightforward stuff.

Conviction

Another of John's characteristics was his strong sense of conviction about the things he believed in. This was particularly evident in four areas.

First, there was reality. Symbolism was common in the society of John's day. He was involved in some of it—his very name suggests that. It was not John the Episcopalian or John the Methodist—but John the Baptist. When he required the people to confess their sin and repent of it, he demanded that they show some evidence of repentance. One of the ways they did this was by being symbolically baptized in water. "But," John said, "don't get confused about this. I baptize you with water, but the one who is coming after me will baptize you with fire and with the Holy Ghost." He was implying that our symbolic acts are not that important. The crux of the matter is the attitude of the heart—that's reality.

Second, John had definite convictions about hypocrisy. He confronted the Pharisees and Sadducees and other hypocrites who came to him: "You generation of vipers, what are you doing here? You snakes!" That's a real man, according to Jesus. He was totally frank with them because he recognized their hypocrisy, play-acting, and preoccupation with externals. Out of deep conviction, he repudiated their apathy about their lack of repentance, confession, and a thorough conversion of their lives.

Third, John had convictions about integrity. Jesus himself took note of it. He said in effect, "All you folks who went out to the Jordan or out into the wilderness to see John the Baptist and hear him speak, what did you expect to see? A reed blowing gently in the breeze, swayed by this opinion and that? One who wouldn't ruffle the water or rock the boat? Or did you go to see a man dressed in fine clothes, enjoying the very best of everything, and living high on the hog? Is that what you went to see? Well, you were surprised, weren't you? Because John wasn't concerned about fine clothes, and he wasn't a reed swayed by every breeze of opinion. Instead, you found that John was committed to integrity, righteousness, and truth—qualities of a real man."

The fourth area of John's convictions was purity. Perhaps the best way to illustrate this is to recall his interaction with King Herod and his wife, Herodias. Herod's power was evidenced by the fact that he eventually had John beheaded. One day John talked to Herod while his wife was present, and what he had to say did not sit well with Herodias.

He said, "King Herod, you're married to Herodias, and it's not right. Herodias was married to your brother Philip, but you and Herodias went to Rome and had an affair. You broke up your brother's marriage, got a divorce, and then went through this improper new marriage. It's not right, and I'm telling you so to your face."

John was utterly convinced that Herod's lifestyle and the sensuality of his court were wrong—and he backed up his convictions with courage. Morality and purity were important to him. He stood firm and spoke out about them. This brings us to another of John's characteristics.

Courage

Because John had convictions about reality, about hypocrisy, about integrity, and about purity, he spoke out against the immorality of

Herod and Herodias. He allowed his convictions to govern his actions, and he dared to challenge evil and evildoers. His attitude was: Some things are good and some are evil; the evil needs to be exposed and the good encouraged. The reformer Martin Luther acted in the same manner, allowing his convictions to govern his deeds. Fifteen centuries after John the Baptist, Luther said, "Here I stand. I can do no other." It takes courage to confront evil wherever it appears, whether in the workplace, the business world, or marriage—courage to confront it in our children, in our social circles, and among our friends. But that's what real men do, according to Jesus.

Because of his courage and conviction, John dared to confront evil in high places. But he also was quite specific about what was good. It's one thing to knock evil; it's an entirely different matter to forthrightly proclaim what is good. John was deeply committed to the teaching of righteousness. And he was able to digest these teachings and apply them to the society of his day.

Vision

The fifth characteristic that qualified John as a real man was his vision. In describing him, Jesus had asked, "When you went out to John the Baptist in the wilderness, what did you expect to see? A reed blowing in the wind or a man dressed in fine clothing? No," he went on, "you went to see a prophet. And that is exactly what you saw—a prophet."

What is a prophet? In Jesus' day a prophet was also called a seer—a person who sees. A seer looks past the immediate to the ultimate. He has been given the perspective of God himself and is able to see the meaning behind events. Unfortunately, because we are committed to the cult of immediacy, in the fast pace of our modern day we often do not realize the consequences of what we do. All we are interested in is an immediate solution to a present problem. That is why cosmetic firms are doing so well. As long as we look good, we are likely to feel good about ourselves; nothing else matters.

So we need to develop the ability to see the consequences of our actions—to see past the immediate to the ultimate. We need this not just for ourselves, but also to be able to help other people see the eternal consequences of their actions. We need to see with the eyes of the one who sits on the throne in heaven. Not only must we think in terms of "now"; we also need to think in terms of "then."

A seer has a vision for possibilities. He or she looks through the situation and envisions how it can glorify God, looking past people's exterior to discover what is really making them tick. The seer is a real man, the kind of gifted person we need in our families, homes, work places, and society.

Unfortunately, we've bought into a lie. What really matters is not so much whether I look or feel good, but whether I am good. The true seer can see past the cosmetic (looking good); he can see through the feeling good; and he can concentrate on the issues that determine whether we are good or evil. This was the vision of John the Baptist, and it has to be the vision of anyone who claims to be a real man.

Vulnerability

John's vulnerability came to light during a very important experience in his life—his imprisonment after he had confronted Herod and Herodias. As he sat there in his cell, his disciples kept visiting him and bringing reports of what Jesus was saying and doing. He then began to doubt his calling and wonder if he had been mistaken. So he asked his disciples, "Would you go back to Jesus and ask him a question for me? Would you ask him if he is really the Messiah? Is he really the one we are looking for, or are we looking for another?"

What an interesting insight this gives us into the mind of John the Baptist. In his doubt, he reveals a winsome vulnerability.

According to research, the five most difficult statements for the modern man to make are: (1) I don't know; (2) I was wrong; (3) I need help; (4) I'm afraid; and (5) I'm sorry. In other words, according to the world's definition, real men do not admit any vulnerability. And if they do, their masculinity is in question. But John was not afraid to admit his vulnerability.

Let's bring this idea closer to home. A lady has been driving with her husband and has a feeling that he has taken a wrong turn. So she mentions it to him. She knows he's touchy about such matters, so she tries to suggest it diplomatically, saying something like, "Dear, I think perhaps you know a better way, a route they haven't put on the maps yet."

How does the husband handle that?

"No," he replies, "I know where I am going." Thirty, forty, or fifty miles later, he notices that for some strange reason the sun has decided to set in the north! Now he is sure his wife knows perfectly well that he's lost. The thing for him to say is, "Honey, I don't know where we are. I was absolutely wrong. When you suggested that I had taken a wrong turn and I said that I had not, you were right! Frankly, I need help."

But the "real man" of the popular caricature is more likely to say, "These dumb maps. You can't rely on them anymore." Or, "Those kids have been out making trouble again. They've switched all those signposts around." Then the wife says, "Don't you think we should go into a filling station and ask?"

Our "real man" is likely to respond: "Why would we need to go into a filling station and ask? I can figure this out myself. Do you want to ask that dummy pumping gas? If he were so sharp, he wouldn't be pumping gas!"

Why do scenes like this occur? In my opinion, our culture has very carefully programmed men not to be vulnerable. We're supposed to hide our feelings, not come to grips with who we really are, and not be honest about ourselves. We can laugh about incidents such as I've described, but I believe that a contributing factor to many of our society's ills is its false conception of what a real man is. A real man demonstrates sincerity and simplicity, courage and conviction, vision and vulnerability. He can look directly at others and say: "I don't know." "I might have been wrong." "I'm afraid." "I need help." That's vulnerability!

There is a marked difference between this kind of honest, humble vulnerability and some of the modern variations on the vulnerable theme. I am not talking about the endless soul-searching of those who appear addicted to a therapeutic method whereby they constantly explore their feelings. Nor am I speaking of the vulnerability that re-casts man as victim. No doubt many men are victims as well as victimizers; but once the mind is set in the victim mode, it is well nigh impossible for people, men or women, to see themselves objectively as divinely created, divinely loved, but desperately sinful people who need to face up to what they really are in the divine reckoning.

John the Baptist's vulnerability is shown in two ways—his honesty and his humility. His humility is unbelievable. One of his best known statements was in reference to Jesus: "He must become greater; I must become less" (John 3:30). Do you remember the circumstances? John was a prophet, and the crowds had been flocking to hear him. Then some people said to him, "Don't you realize that the crowds are rushing to see Jesus?"

He said, "Sure, I realize that. I sent some of them over myself, because I must go on decreasing and he is the one who must go on increasing."

There's nothing phony about John's humility—it's real. He has come to grips with who he really is in relation to Jesus. A humble man is not afraid to admit who he is. Such a man admits openly, "I must go on decreasing. He must go on increasing."

Various symbols illustrate the relationship between Jesus and John the Baptist. Jesus was the Light; John the Baptist was the lamp. John was the medium through whom Jesus did his work. On one occasion, John said to his disciples as Jesus walked past, "Look, the Lamb of God, who takes away the sin of the world!" (John 1:29). Jesus was the Way; John the Baptist was the signpost. Jesus was the Message; John was the messenger. Jesus was the Word; John was the voice.

John didn't like to talk about himself. His main concern was to understand himself in the light of who Jesus Christ is. When we come to terms with who we are compared to Jesus Christ, we find it's not too difficult to be humble.

Clement Atlee, one of Winston Churchill's greatest foes, rarely heard a good word from Churchill. But on one occasion, to everyone's amazement, Churchill said: "Atlee is a very humble man." Then he added, "Of course, he has a lot to be humble about."

Our problem, when we compare ourselves with Jesus, is that we have a lot to be humble about. And our humility shouldn't be surprising. Unfortunately, our humility usually lies beneath the surface, because to be humble is to be vulnerable.

John's vulnerability was also reflected in his honesty. He was honest about his doubts as he sat there in his prison cell. Why did he wonder if Jesus really was the Messiah? He must have thought, *If Jesus is the Messiah, why doesn't he get me out of this place? The Messiah is supposed to release the captives, isn't he?* John was honest about his doubts and fears.

The book *The Friendless American Male* discusses the man who has no real relationship with anyone—the kind of relationship that would allow him to be honest and genuine with others. Why does this happen? Because to develop that kind of friendship requires a certain degree of honesty and vulnerability that is lacking in many men.

We follow all kinds of models today, whether it be Lee Iacocca, the latest Heisman Trophy winner, or some actor or rock star. They may or may not have qualities that we admire. We can't go wrong, however, if we select a model who had the imprimatur of Jesus: John the Baptist. Jesus said there was not a greater man born of woman.

An enigmatic phrase concludes Jesus' statement about John. "Among those born of women there is no one greater than John; yet the one who is least in the kingdom of God is greater than he" (Luke 7:28). Even "the least in the kingdom" is greater than he? What does Jesus mean? Here he seems to be saying, "Look at all the qualities of manhood and remember that these are only secondary. The primary objective is to make sure you are part of the kingdom." One could exhibit all the greatest male characteristics in the world and still miss the kingdom. A real man is part of the kingdom and acknowledges the King. He has come to repentance, is open to confession, and proves the reality of his repentance by his converted lifestyle. In addition, he has begun to display all the characteristics of real manhood. That's the kind of person we are looking for.

If we had to identify a model of a real man, who would it be? And if we define a real man in terms of this model, are we seeing these qualities develop in our own lives? Finally, if we don't define a real man in these terms, where are we getting our ideas of manhood? And how valid are they? What is a real man? Take a close look at John the Baptist for the answer.

Let's Get Practical

1. What definitions of manhood have you been given by your family? By your peers?

2. How have society's various definitions of manhood bothered, discouraged, or angered you? What truths from the Bible can remedy these faulty definitions?

3. What qualities of John the Baptist's manhood are particularly challenging to you? Which ones encourage you?

4. Which of these qualities—sincerity, simplicity, conviction, courage, vision, and vulnerability—have developed most strongly in you? Which of these qualities need further development in your life?

5. If you are a man, how will you build true manhood into your lifestyle and attitudes?

2

The Real World Needs Real Women

As a pastor I am especially aware that women make up at least 60 percent of the church's work force. Without women, most churches would cease to function, and world missions might grind to a halt.

However, have you noticed how dramatically society has been shifting in its attitude toward women in recent years? How are we to regard these changes? As a Christian I believe that, although I'm called to actively live in my culture, I must subject it to the searchlight of the Scriptures. Admittedly, it's much easier to ignore the Bible and live by the dictates of our culture, as most people are doing. As a pastor and a servant of the living God, I have a responsibility to minister in this culture. In that role, I believe that I (and all Christians) must be concerned about what is happening to women in our culture.

More than thirty years ago Betty Friedan wrote *The Feminine Mystique*, a book powerful in its impact and influence. It launched the feminist movement, radical elements of which are still alive and well today. In the book, Friedan pinpoints the problem for women today as being a crisis in identity. What does Friedan mean by a "crisis in identity"? She points out that the role of modern women is changing. Many women today are wondering who and what they are. Should they be traditionalists or feminists? Friedan contends that our culture has stunted the development of women and deprived them of opportunities to be themselves. This stunting has directly contributed to what she calls "the feminine mystique." That is, if you give a woman a good man, some handsome kids, and a nice home, she'll be fulfilled. But there is far more to a woman's fulfillment, says Friedan. Today's woman is looking outside the home for fulfillment, and if she isn't allowed to break out of that mystique, she is likely to have a major problem with her identity. In that sense, I agree with Friedan and the many other writers, sociologists, and activists who have since voiced similar concerns.

The question before us then is: When we look at real women, what is the issue? Is it a matter of the feminine mystique, or is it all a monumental female mistake? In the remainder of the chapter we will attempt to answer that question by examining woman's identity as (1) revealed in Creation, (2) obscured in the Fall, and (3) renewed in redemption.

Woman's Identity Revealed in Creation

In Genesis 1 God said, "Let us make man in our image, in our likeness, and let them rule over the fish of the sea and the birds of the air, over the livestock, over all the earth, and over all the creatures that move along the ground" (v. 26, NIV).

Verse 27 amplifies that statement: "So God created man in his own image, in the image of God he created him; male and female he created them."

The basic features of woman's identity are clearly established at Creation. First, she is equal with the male as a created being. When God said, "Let us create man," he didn't say, "Let us create males." He said, "Let us create man, male and female."

The second feature of woman's identity noted in this creation passage is that she is a bearer of the divine image. Mankind as created in the image of God was male and female.

In what sense is the female in the image of God? Various answers can be given to that question. One idea is that God has revealed himself in terms of his attributes, which are both masculine and feminine. Recently, feminists have gone overboard on this idea—even wanting us to rewrite the Bible and to pray, "Our Mother who art in heaven." This, of course, is unacceptable because it imposes our own perspective on Scripture. When we consider God's attributes, we can clearly see that Scripture sometimes describes him in feminine terms. One example is when Jesus said, "I have longed to gather your children together, as a hen gathers her chicks under her wings" (Luke 13:34, NIV).

When the Bible teaches that both men and women are made in the divine image, it suggests to me that both male and female demonstrate divine attributes. It could also mean that in their relationship to each other, male and female are modeling relationships that exist in the Trinity between Father, Son, and Holy Spirit. Whatever it may mean, this statement is unequivocal: Woman is as much a bearer of the divine image as man.

Verse 28 emphasizes the third and fourth features of woman's identity. It reads: "God blessed them and said to them, 'Be fruitful and increase in number; fill the earth and subdue it. Rule over the fish of the sea and the birds of the air and over every living creature that moves on the ground.'" Notice the third feature here. Woman and man were equally blessed by God. He enabled and equipped them to be and do all that he required of them.

Fourth, in verse 28 woman and man received a joint commission from God. They shared God's mandate to mankind to rule and preside over the entire earth. Woman was to be an equal partner in this commission—a vital part of her identity.

In Genesis 2—a somewhat different but complementary account of creation—we are introduced to the fifth feature of woman's identity. In chapter 1, God generally describes creation in terms of male and female as its pinnacle in the image of God, subduing and ruling the earth. In chapter 2, however, he deals with the creation of mankind in more detail and presents man as the focal point: "The LORD God said, 'It is not good for the man to be alone. I will make a helper suitable for him'" (v. 18, NIV).

The expression "It is not good" comes in stark contrast to what has been said so far. All through chapter 1, when God created things, he looked at them and evaluated them as "good" and "very good." Now, suddenly something is "not good." The Lord looks at man and says, "No good." What is no good about him? It is not good that he should be alone, and so God decides to make him a helper—the final feature of woman's identity revealed in creation.

This action by God has been interpreted in many ways. One little girl was asked to write an essay on why there were so many women in the world. Her essay went basically like this. In the beginning God created man. After looking at him, God said, "I can do better than that," so he made woman. After he had made woman, he was so convinced that she was better he decided, *I'll make a whole lot more of them.* And that's why there are so many more women than men in the world! There are some people who might agree with her.

The sexual equality described in Genesis 1 must be worked out in practical terms. This brings us to the term "suitable helper," used to describe woman in Genesis 2:18. What does this word mean?

Many people, particularly men, think a helper is someone who exists to take care of their every need. There is a sense in which woman is made for man in this context, but not in terms of subservience. The word translated "helper" is quite common in the Old Testament and frequently is used to describe God in his relationship to Israel. If the idea of helper is that of an automatic, subservient role, we come up with the ludicrous notion of God being subservient to Israel. This is utter nonsense!

The correct idea of "suitable helper" is that of an ideal one who comes alongside to help someone who cannot function alone. Could Israel function without Jehovah? No. Jehovah, the helper, came alongside and enabled Israel to function. So if mankind is to function, the ideal male and female must be brought together by God in partnership. They must be uniquely equipped, blessed, commissioned, and called by God as his created beings, in his image, to do all that he has willed for them.

Let's take a closer look now at woman's creation. In Genesis 2 we see that woman as man's helper is not only made for man; she is also made from man. For Adam, no suitable helper was found. So the Lord God caused the man to fall into a deep sleep; and while he was sleeping, he took one of the man's ribs and closed up the place with flesh. Then the Lord God made a woman from the rib he had taken out of man, and he brought her to the man. The man said, "This is now bone of my bones and flesh of my flesh; she shall be called woman [*isha*], for she was taken out of man [*ish*]" (Gen. 2:23, NIV).

There is an obvious connection between the Hebrew words *ish* and *isha*—a wonderful connection! In contrast to everything else that had been created, woman was taken from man. All other creatures had been formed from the dust of the earth, but woman was unique in being created from the side of man. This sets her apart from all other created beings.

Some people have argued that because woman was made from man, she is in some way or other inferior to him. But man was made from the dust of the earth. Are we to conclude that he is inferior to dust?

The Bible's message is that, in marked contrast to the rest of creation, woman is uniquely called alongside man to be a coheir. This is woman's identity as revealed in creation.

Woman's Identity Obscured in the Fall

Someone may ask, "If everything was so great for women in the beginning, why are we in such a mess now?" I must admit that women are discriminated against in our society. For example, as soon as they are divorced or widowed, they are often looked upon as needing "a man to look after them." Somehow women are generally regarded as inferior. Let's look at one of the reasons for this.

In a sense, woman's loss of identity began to occur at the Fall. The early verses of Genesis 3 relate how the serpent deceived the woman.

"Did God really say that you should not eat from any tree in the Garden?" asked the serpent (v. 1).

The woman dutifully replied, "We may eat from some of the trees in the Garden, but God did say that we must not eat of a certain one or we will surely die" (v. 2).

The serpent said, "You won't die. For God knows when you eat of it your eyes will be open; you will be like God, knowing good and evil" (v. 4-5). So the woman ate and gave the forbidden fruit to her husband, and he ate some as well (v. 6).

Then, in verse 13, when the Lord God asked the woman, "What have you done?" she replied, "the serpent deceived me and I ate."

How was the woman deceived? The answer lies in verse 6: "When the woman saw that the fruit of the tree was good for food, and that it was pleasant to the eye, and a tree to be desired to make one wise, she took of the fruit thereof, and did eat, and gave to her husband." Her interests were in goodness, pleasure, and wisdom, and we probably shouldn't condemn her for that. Her problem—a common one to both men and women—was that she desired these things independent of God. This was her mistake.

Why was she deceived? She was deceived because she was confronted by the craftiest, wisest part of God's creation. She was deceived because she was out of her league—totally outclassed. When she explained to God that she was deceived, that was the end of it. He didn't question her any further.

On the other hand, her husband wasn't deceived. He simply went along with what his wife was saying, because he wanted to be happy and make her happy. He was more concerned with immediate gratification than he was with obeying God.

This brings up an interesting point concerning Adam and Eve. We do not know how much God had told Eve, how much she really knew. But we do know what God had told Adam. Eve was confronted by Satan himself; Adam wasn't. That's why the Bible reports that Eve was deceived, but that Adam caused the whole race to fall.

The deception and fall brought problems into the world. God had said to them, "If you disobey me, if you try to live independently of me, the day you do, you'll die." They didn't die physically the day they disobeyed him, but they were spiritually estranged from God. This introduced a principle of physical death, which issued eventually into eternal death. The wages of sin, Paul tells us in Romans, is death—eternal, physical, and spiritual alienation from God. Death was now experienced by all mankind. How does the Fall, this new experience of deadness, affect women?

The answer is found in Genesis 3:16 (NIV): God said to the woman, "I will greatly increase your pains in childbearing; with pain you will give birth to children. Your desire will be for your husband, and he will rule over you." This verse points out two effects of the Fall on women. The first is that woman will experience suffering. Suffering, of course, is a reminder of death. Healthy people do not talk and think much about death. Death is on the minds of those who are ill. Pain, suffering, and death are related.

This is the ultimate irony. In the woman's unique capacity to reproduce life lies the reminder of death, for the very life that she reproduces is brought forth in pain, the precursor of death itself.

The second effect on woman is in the latter part of verse 16. God says, "Your desire will be for your husband, and he will rule over you." As a result of the Fall, woman will not only experience suffering; she will experience subjugation as well. This brief sentence contains real food for thought.

The problem here is uncertainty over the exact meaning of the word translated "desire." It literally means "turning toward." Some have interpreted this as woman's desire for affection and romance, for intimacy with a man. Other people say, "No, it suggests that women will 'turn toward' men in an aggressive, antagonistic way." There are other variations on this theme, and that's part of the problem.

Another aspect of the problem in interpretation is deciding whether this sentence is *prescriptive* or *descriptive*. Perhaps God is saying, "All right, woman, you did this; therefore you will be cursed. You will desire your husband, but he will rule over you— and it's your own fault. It's part of the curse." In this interpretation, the sentence is prescriptive: God is prescribing it.

On the other hand, God may be saying, "As a result of what you have done, all mankind will get fouled up. Relationships will become a mess, especially between men and women. And women will particularly be affected by male abuse and domination." Paul wrote: "Now I want you to realize that the head of every man is Christ, and the head of the woman is man, and the head of Christ is

God" (1 Cor. 11:3, NIV). Those who hold to a "descriptive" interpretation of Genesis 3:16 believe that the Fall so perverted this "headship" that it has degenerated into all manner of confusing and inappropriate relations between the sexes, with woman the chief victim. So some commentators say God was simply describing what would happen. However this sentence is intended to be understood, let me remind you of one thing—we spend a lot time and energy trying to cope with the effects of the Fall.

What do we do for women in the pain of childbirth? Do we say, "Serves you right. It's all part of the Fall"? What do we say to the gardener when the thorns and thistles come up? Do we say, "Serves you right. It's a result of the Fall"? What do we say to the man who is overburdened at work? Do we say, "Serves you right"?

No, we don't say any of these things. To the woman in childbirth, we give an anesthetic. We give the gardener a weed killer. We supply the overburdened worker with computers and machines. And to the woman who doesn't like housekeeping, we give all kinds of helpful appliances: blenders, mixers, and things that go bump in the night.

What are all these devices designed to do? They are intended to alleviate the consequences of the Fall. If that is true (and we believe that man's domination of woman is a consequence of the Fall), then we should be doing all that we can to ease those consequences. What conclusion do we come to?

From my point of view, woman was a magnificent creation, but as a result of the Fall, she was placed in a subservient role, far removed from the God's intention at creation. If that is indeed the case, the question is, What are Christians and the Christian church doing about it?

Let me illustrate this idea of subservience. In Genesis, God very clearly said that a man would leave his father and mother and be united to his wife (one man to one woman). But what happened? Before long the old patriarchs had wives coming out of their ears! And what they expected of their wives demonstrates that women were in a subservient role during patriarchal times. This was never God's intention. It is a consequence of the Fall, man behaving toward woman in a way far removed from what God had ordained in Genesis 1 and 2.

What does history teach us? The philosopher Aristotle (384-322 B.C.) considered woman to be a kind of mutilated male. His opinions affected later philosophers and even church leaders such as Thomas Aquinas, the Roman Catholic philosopher and theologian who said, "As regards the individual nature, woman is defective and misbegotten. For the active force in the male seed tends to the production of a perfect likeness in the masculine sex. While the production of women comes from a defect." In other words, a perfect male seed produces a boy; a defective male seed produces a girl!

What about other men who were helping to formulate Christian theology? Martin Luther, for example, is quoted as saying, "If a woman becomes weary or dead from childbearing, it matters not. She is there to do it."

Perhaps this partially explains why people in the secular world are sometimes angry at the church. Our history won't bear too careful an investigation at times.

This belief in woman's inferiority has been expressed by the major religions. For example, the Hindus believe in reincarnation—that when you die, you return to earth as something else. When a baby girl is born, Hindus say to themselves, *Ah! This woman is a reincarnation of a higher form that did something bad. She has been reincarnated as a woman as punishment.*

Buddhism teaches a similar message. Gautama said, "Women are evil, jealous, and stupid. Avoid the sight of them, and do not speak to them."

The Islamic Koran teaches: "Allah had made one [man] superior to the other [woman] . . . admonish them, send them to beds apart, and beat them."

Judaism says this: "Every man who teaches his daughter the Torah is as if he teaches her promiscuity. Better to burn the Torah than to teach it to a woman."

Without question, both religious and secular history have borne out the "curse" described by God at the Fall. If we project this kind of thinking into our present day, can we consider it as part of the residual consequences of the Fall? Is this the reason that, as Friedan put it, women have a problem with their identity? I believe the church could be a tremendous help to many women if we could teach them the truth about their identity à la creation—and show them how it was obscured in the Fall.

Woman's Identity Renewed in Redemption

What was the intention of God in redemption, and did it involve women? Unquestionably, he had a number of intentions, among them (1) to counteract the effects of the Fall, and (2) to restore the created order. In terms of woman having a role in redemption, we cannot avoid this fact: At the very time God was outlining what would happen to women in the Fall, he also made the great redemptive statement that the seed of the woman would bruise the serpent's head (Gen. 3:15).

There is a bright and shining ray of hope for women in this declaration of their intimate involvement in the plan of redemption. This leads us to the positive effects of the redemption of woman's identity.

First, let's consider how woman's identity was renewed in the promise of the new covenant. In Acts 2, the apostle Peter, speaking on the day of Pentecost, reminded the people that this outpouring of the Spirit was the direct fulfillment of Joel 2:28: "I will pour out my Spirit on all people. Your sons and daughters will prophesy" (NIV). It was a fulfillment of the new covenant in the sense that God's Spirit was poured out upon both men and women. Men and women were shown once again to be equal in terms of blessing and opportunity.

The apostle Paul speaks to this same issue in Galatians 3:28: "There is neither Jew nor Greek, slave nor free, male nor female, for you are all one in Christ Jesus" (NIV). This is a great statement of Christian liberty, especially in the context of Jewish religion. The Orthodox Jew, in his daily liturgy, often thanked God that he was not a Gentile, or a slave, or a woman. Now Paul is telling the

Galatian Christians that in Christ there is no discrimination.

This is a very powerful statement. The immediate question is, How does it fit into the whole context of biblical interpretation? F. F. Bruce, often considered the dean of conservative evangelical scholars, believes that Paul is articulating a basic principle in this verse and that all of his other statements concerning women are to be understood in relation to it, and not vice versa. In other words, when you look at what Paul says about women, consider Galatians 3:28 as his final word.

In writing to Timothy, Paul said, "I do not permit a woman to teach or to have authority over a man" (1 Tim. 2:12, NIV). He also says in this verse, "She must be silent." Paul also told the women to keep their heads covered because "the head of the woman is man" (1 Cor. 11:3, NIV).

How do we square these apparent contradictions? On the one hand, Paul seems to be saying there is no difference—"There is neither male nor female." On the other hand, he is saying, "There is no difference except for the differences."

Bruce gives us a helpful principle to follow here. He suggests that there is neither male nor female in the redemptive economy of God; that when Paul's writings seem to restrict women, they are to be considered on the basis that no fundamental difference or discrimination is allowed. Because this is the main issue, we need to look at Paul's commands in the light of the society he was addressing.

In requiring women to be silent in the church, Paul was apparently trying to restore order to a disorderly church. When we look at what he says about not allowing a woman to teach or exercise authority over a man, we notice that it is authoritative teaching he will not allow. Today's teaching in the church is quite different from the teaching in Paul's day. The only teaching that is valid now comes under the authority of Scripture. Teaching then didn't come under the authority of Scripture, because there wasn't a New Testament.

In essence, Bruce's clarifying message is this: "In redemption, there is a renewed position for women of equality, or opportunity, or privilege, or blessing. They are to find their identity in these things."

Now let's look at the renewing effect of Jesus' behavior and attitude on woman's identity. Jesus' treatment of women was radical and revolutionary, to say the least. He acted contrary to the norm wherever he went. For instance, he used women as examples of righteousness and told stories about them to men, saying to them, in effect, "There you are; there's righteousness." That was a new experience for men who regarded women as inferior and irrelevant.

Do you recall his interaction with Martha and Mary? Martha was doing the woman's work—and woman's work is in the kitchen, right? Mary, however, was sitting at Jesus' feet in a Bible study. All upset, Martha said, "Tell her to come and do her job." Jesus replied, "Mary has chosen the better part." This was a radical statement by Jesus for the times.

Women in those days were regarded as so seductive that if they appeared in public with their hair unbraided or uncovered, they were promptly divorced—no questions asked. One night when Jesus was at dinner, reclining on a couch, a woman of doubtful reputation came in. Everyone present knew her and said, "Ah. We'll soon see if he is a prophet or not. He'll see through her." The woman started to cry and washed Jesus' feet with her tears. Then she uncovered her hair and used it to wipe his feet. And Jesus allowed her to do it. The onlookers were shocked.

What was Jesus' attitude toward women as witnesses? Take note that women were not considered valid witnesses in a court of law at that time. Well, Jesus knew that women were the only witnesses of his death because the men had fled. And who were the first witnesses to the empty tomb and the resurrection? Women! Jesus presented women as reliable witnesses and sought to restore their identity.

Scripture is unequivocal about woman's identity in creation. Jesus explained how life became all mixed up because of the Fall, but redemption brought the tremendous power of God into play. It can undo the awesome consequences of the Fall and restore people to the position of God's original intent for them. Where does this leave us in terms of woman's identity today?

The Contemporary Challenge

Let me suggest a plan of action. Many women need to look very carefully at their identity, examining whether they perceive themselves as persons uniquely created and redeemed by God. They need to identify the consequences of the Fall in their lives and find out to what extent the Lord Jesus and the power of redemption has set them free.

Men, on the other hand, need to take a hard look at their attitudes toward women. A number of years ago I received the shock of my life. I was invited to have lunch with several godly, active women of our church. There was not a radical among them. For about two hours I listened to them. It was a total eye-opener for me, an utter shock. They weren't troublemakers. They were godly, beautiful women, deeply involved in serving the Lord Jesus, committed to their families, and thoroughly obeying God. But they had some surprising things to say! As a man I realized how unconcerned and uncaring I had been with regard to women in general, and women in the church in particular.

They expressed appreciation for the measure of freedom to minister which they had been granted, but pointed out that they were never invited to exercise some gifts with which they had been spiritually endowed. They pointed out that on the rare occasion the church bothered to consider how and what women felt, the discussion had included all males and women had not even been consulted. And they also spoke of the patronizing (bordering on insulting!) way in which they were treated by men if they ever voiced the slightest concern. I repeat that these women were not complainers or troublemakers; they were classy, godly, committed believers. Fortunately they were able to open my eyes, and to a certain extent I have been able to share with others what I have learned on this score. But there is still a long way to go.

I think that one of the great opportunities for the Christian church at the present time is to listen to women in this age of confusion about women and their roles. We must begin to help them see that they are making some valid points about inequities in the church. But when it becomes a radical form of feminism—which is simply women united against men—then we must be careful.

Radical feminism says, "Men are free to do as they like with their bodies; women are free to do as they like with their bodies; therefore, we have the inalienable right to abort whenever we wish. And we're certainly not going to allow men to tell us what we can and cannot do!" This kind of thinking has sent shock waves through the church, and rightly so. But we should not put our fingers in our ears because some women have taken extreme, unacceptable positions. When thinking women begin to point out the gross injustices toward women in the church and society and call attention to the biblical position, we need to take notice. Those of us who really want to follow God had better stand up with the dissenters where their dissent is biblically legitimate and support them.

Many hurt, disillusioned, bitter women are very reachable if Christians will go to them and simply explain woman's identity in creation, in the Fall, and in redemption. I think that is another way we can communicate the liberating impact of the gospel of Christ to a hurting world. Christ's command "Go ye into all the world" includes the mandate to minister to the hurting women in our world.

Let's Get Practical

1. What do you think is most difficult about being a woman in your family? In your church? In society in general?

2. What does the Creation story tell you about what it means to be a woman? What has society told you that is contrary to what Creation reveals?

3. If you are a woman, what effects of the Fall do you feel most severely, and how do you handle it? If you are a man, what are you presently doing to help reverse those effects?

4. What does it mean for a woman to be redeemed by the death and resurrection of the Lord Jesus Christ? How can redemption reverse the results of the Fall that particularly relate to women?

5. How can you apply the results of the redemption to your life right now?

3

The Marriage That Makes It

Have you ever heard the expression, "That marriage was made in heaven"? Over years in the pastorate, I've performed a host of weddings, and I must admit, occasionally I've thought that—very occasionally! However, being a rather realistic person, I'm more inclined to ask, "If marriages are made in heaven, why are so many of them failing, even among Christians?"

By this time, the statistics have become almost monotonous: Almost one of every two marriages is ending up in divorce in the United States. Lurking beneath the statistics is the fact that many couples are enduring a marriage in name only for the sake of children or society's approval. The statistics also do not include the increasing numbers of men and women who are not even bothering to get married, but are just living together. Those couples now number in the millions.

That's why I think it's important for us to find out what Jesus has to say about real marriages. One of his teachings is found in Mark 10:1-2, where, interestingly enough, his comments on marriage are made in the context of a question about divorce. Seeking to trick Jesus, some Pharisees asked him, "Is it lawful for a man to divorce his wife?" (v. 2, NIV). People are still asking that question, and books have been written, seeking the answer. But Jesus' questioners were trying to trap him in a big argument that was going on in Israel.

Even though they wanted Jesus to talk about divorce, he began with simple statements about marriage. In a society in which divorce is becoming more and more prevalent, the big question we should be discussing and debating is not divorce. Our urgent need is to articulate again and again what the Scriptures teach about marriage.

Notice how succinctly Jesus responds: "At the beginning of creation 'God made them male and female.' 'For this reason a man will leave his father and mother and be united to his wife, and the two will become one flesh.' So they are no longer two, but one. Therefore what God has joined together, let man not separate" (vv. 6-9, NIV).

In these brief sentences Jesus gives us his thoughts on the subject of marriage. This passage is not exhaustive of Jesus' teaching on the subject, but it is the basis for our discussion of real marriage. For the remainder of the chapter, we will be considering fundamental principles that must be incorporated into marriage if it is to be real.

Marriage Is a Divine Institution

First, marriage is a divine institution. The Pharisees wanted Jesus to talk about divorce, specifically hoping he would disagree with the teaching of Moses. Instead, he took them back to a time before Moses—the very beginning of Creation. In doing so, Jesus was emphasizing an important fact. Our biblical model for marriage goes back to the very beginning of time.

Every society we've ever explored recognizes some form of marriage. Even the most primitive societies have some sort of legislation, some sort of rules regulating family life. However, this is not what I'm talking about. We do not base our understanding of marriage on contemporary human legislation. We go back to what God has said from the very beginning of Creation.

Our modern tendency is to look at what our state or federal law allows us to do. We tend to base our behavior on commonly accepted norms. All these may or may not be valid, but they are of secondary significance at best. Of primary significance is what God has said from the beginning of Creation. Let's consider some of his basic laws.

God has built physical laws into his creation. And if we ignore them, we suffer the consequences. For example, if I decide that the natural laws governing heat don't operate and I put my hand in the fire, I will nonetheless be burned. If I disregard the laws of gravity and decide to jump off a seventh-floor balcony, I will make quite a splash when I land. We cannot disregard God's physical laws with impunity.

By the same token, God has built sociological, theological, and psychological laws into us from Creation, and we can no more disregard these laws with impunity than we can physical laws. Disobeying God's fundamental laws—psychological, theological, and sociological—will only do us harm.

Marriage is not a human institution—something dreamed up by humanity. Therefore, alternate lifestyles, as we call them, cannot be valid if they are counter to God's Word. That is why I begin this chapter by treating marriage as an institution of God, not humans. Marriage is ordained by God for the welfare of human society. There are three reasons for this.

Psychological reasons for marriage

According to psychologists and psychiatrists, we human beings need to receive and to express love. We suffer severe psychological trauma if these needs are not fulfilled, as they are fundamental to our human psyche. But where are we to learn to love and be loved? Where are we to see love modeled and take those first steps of risking love? The answer, of course, is in the family. And if we do not have a solid family situation, there is a very high probability that we will be deficient in our own experience of love and the ability to express it. What makes the family a secure place, where we can learn to love and be loved? A secure marriage builds the foundation for the family. That's why God ordained it. If we disregard the importance of marriage and family, we will be doing extreme psychological damage to everybody concerned. It should not surprise us, therefore, that many of the disturbed people in our society are the products of broken homes and broken marriages.

Sociological reasons for marriage

John Donne told us that no man is an island. We know that! No man lives unto himself. No woman lives unto herself. We do not live in a vacuum. Whatever we do affects somebody else. We are sociological as well as psychological creatures. The question is, How do we learn to function properly in a society so full of people who do not know how to relate to others?

The family provides an opportunity for us to learn how to relate to others. If their parents are functioning properly, children very quickly learn the meaning of authority. And they soon learn from brothers and sisters that they are not the only pebbles on the beach. They learn to give, to take, to adjust. They learn that the same people who dirty dishes are capable of washing them. Thus social skills are learned in the family. And if the family is falling apart because marriage is failing, society will reap a harvest of misfits.

Theological reasons for marriage

The Old Testament repeatedly uses the idea of marriage to illustrate a theological truth, as does the New Testament. In the Old Testament, God promises or covenants to be our God eternally and invites us to respond by being his family. But we have difficulty grasping that truth, and we need a model or an illustration. The Old Testament uses the model of marriage. In exactly the same way that a man makes a covenant with his wife (and the wife to her husband), God commits himself to his people.

In the New Testament, the marriage model is used to show that Christ is the head, the "husband" of the church, which is his body. Christ so loved the church that he gave himself for it. He is the model husband. We learn this as we study the Scriptures, seeking a model for the divine institution of marriage.

Marriage Recognizes Divinely Ordained Sexuality

Sexuality has been part and parcel of humanity from the very beginning. If we are to grasp the meaning of our humanity, we need to understand our sexuality. This is where the problems arise. Look at what has happened. There is total confusion about sexuality in our day.

Some of our so-called traditional norms no longer work. The old idea of male-dominated marriage is not valid in a world where more than half of the work force is made up of women. The idea of man as "king of his castle" is as outdated as most monarchies in our fast-changing world. Wives and children are no longer expected to submit to a "lord-and-master" mentality, where the husband and father rules like a tyrant.

The "everything-goes" approach is equally invalid. How can you have "open marriage" in a world where AIDS and other sexually transmitted diseases are spreading like wildfire? More and more people are beginning to recognize and recommend the biblical norm of monogamy in a world going mad in its pursuit of pleasurable sex.

If our marriages are to function properly, we cannot base them on traditional norms that have departed from Scripture; nor can we base them on radical concepts that reject Scripture. We must take a closer look at what the Bible teaches about the nature of men and women and how they are to relate to each other. One reason we are having such terrible problems in our marriages is that most of us have not come to grips with a biblical understanding of sexuality.

We preachers are usually not considered very wise in these matters. In fact, we're considered naive and out-of-date by most young people today. But I've been around awhile and have learned some things.

Years ago in England I worked with young people in a coffee-house ministry. I didn't approach them with any kind of a canned talk. I'd simply invite them to talk about what concerned them most. And sex was always at the top of their list.

"Whoever heard of a preacher who believed in sex?" was obviously their attitude. My response was usually very simple: "I'll be very happy to talk to you about sex. It's one of my very favorite subjects, because if it were not for sex I would not be here. If it were not for sex, you would not be here either. Therefore, if it were not for sex, nobody would be here—what a dull meeting that would be!"

When the laughter died down, I would go on: "In fact, the only reason we can have a meeting tonight is because of what?" And they would chorus, "Sex!" Then I would say, "Wonderful. You learn very quickly. Therefore, let's have three cheers for sex!—hip, hip, hooray!" and we would all applaud sex.

After this introduction, I would then say: "Now then, the next thing we notice about sex is that God invented it, and he's not a dirty old man. Therefore, if you want to understand sex and its beauty, fullness, and purity, you had better find out what God says about it." At that point you usually could have heard the proverbial pin drop. They were eager to hear what God had to say then, and I think young people today are just as eager.

To sum up, the second principle of a real marriage is that it incorporates a healthy, biblical grasp of sexuality. We must be willing to reject ideas antithetical to Scripture and be ready to respond to all that God says on the subject. Otherwise, we get into all kinds of trouble.

Marriage Means Commitment

In verse 7 Jesus says, quoting Genesis, "For this reason a man will leave his father and mother and be united to his wife" (NIV). Why would a man have to leave his father and mother? Because "at the beginning of creation God made them male and female."

I know some men who have it pretty good with their fathers and mothers. They are single and well cared for. Somebody does their laundry. They don't even have to pay room and board. They have life by the tail—and then they throw it all away. What do they do? They decide to leave mother and father, giving up all that security, and get married, picking up all the expense of a wife and a home of their own. Why on earth would they do that? Because God, from the very beginning of creation, "created them male and female." A divinely created male felt a response to a divinely created female. If it's right, it is also a divinely created response. For that reason the man chooses to leave the old life and moves into a whole new situation. But notice the key to this. He chooses to leave.

This relates particularly to the society in which Jesus was living and to which he was addressing his remarks. In those days the male left his family to move to the area in which his wife lived for a very simple reason. If anything should happen to him (if he suffered an untimely death), then her father and brothers would care for her. She had no welfare or insurance; her family was her insurance.

Even though the situation is different today, this matter of choice still applies. Marriages often get into difficulty because people do not live out this basic choice. They choose to get married. They choose to leave the single state to become involved in a new situation. Accepting responsibility, they say they will leave the old life. But they don't. Although they say they are willing and prepared to move into this new experience, they look back. They lack commitment because they don't know what the new relationship involves. Marriages fall into all kinds of problems in this area.

Let me illustrate this from a counseling experience I had many years ago when I first came to the United States. One very cold night in November a young couple with whom I'd met for premarital counseling came to my home for a late appointment. As they came in the door, the cold blast of wind outside seemed warm compared to the atmosphere between them. Tactful person that I am, I decided to be diplomatic. So I said, "I see you had a fight on the way over here." After several denials, they finally admitted it. This is what happened:

For many years, the young man had gone deer hunting. I said, "Don't tell me. . . .Your wedding day is on the opening day of deer season."

She looked at me and said, "Right. And you know what he said?"

"Yes. He said you're going to spend your honeymoon deer hunting."

"Yes. Can you believe that?"

I glanced at him and he said, "I go to the symphony with her, don't I?"

I had to do something to defuse the situation, so I said to him, "I think we have a problem here. As I understand it, you feel that your young bride should go and sit up in northern Wisconsin, freezing and shooting deer as part of your honeymoon?"

She interrupted, "Right."

"And you feel that because you've gone to the symphony with her, she should go along with this?" He nodded.

"We've got to compromise, haven't we?" I asked. I turned to her, "Why don't you agree to go with him, and take your tape player and all your tapes of Beethoven and Mozart and Haydn and play them up there in the woods?" Then I looked at him. "How about you taking your rifle to the symphony and seeing if you can bag yourself a cellist?"

By this time they were smiling a little, and we could begin to address the problem. The solution to their problem was not to compromise. Taking Beethoven on a deer-hunting trip was as ridiculous as bringing a rifle to the symphony. That kind of compromise wouldn't work.

This was my counsel to them: "To the best of my knowledge, you don't have to get married. Why are you choosing to get married?" Looking at the man, I said, "If hunting is more important to you than marriage and your wife, why do you need a wife? Stick with deer. The simple fact of the matter is this: If you're going to enter a new relationship, it ought to be because you've chosen that new relationship over the old one."

I'm happy to say the young fellow recognized how unfair he was being, and the couple worked out their differences. Even though they didn't go deer hunting on their honeymoon, they went together later!

The old King James Version renders the rest of Mark 10:7 "and cleave unto his wife." Not only does the man need to be willing to leave; he must also cleave unto her. *Cleave* is an Old English word with many different meanings. It could denote splitting a piece of wood right down the middle. But it could also mean sticking something together. The Greek word here translated "united" or "cleave" is the word for glue. So Jesus is really saying, "When you come into marriage, you are glued together, and you are committed to that gluing." I could put it this way: At the end of a marriage service it would be quite legitimate for the groom to turn to his bride and say, "I am going to stick to you through thick and thin." And she could respond, "Right, and you're stuck with me!" We are emphasizing here that commitment is the bedrock of marriage—a truth that needs to be reiterated in these confusing times.

Our society takes a very sophisticated approach. "We will go into marriage and accept the fact that it's not easy," people say. "It's for mature people, and there's a high possibility we may make a mistake, or we may not be suited to each other. If that is the case, we'll be sensible and adult about it. We'll divide our resources and decide who gets custody of the children. Our lawyers will take care of it, and we'll remain the best of friends."

Sounds great, doesn't it? But what a gross parody and caricature this is of marriage as God ordained it. Let's call it what it is. God intended for us to take our marriage vows seriously. He knew that if we entered marriage with all the attractive options open, we wouldn't bother to work at it. So God, in effect, said, "Make the commitment. Recognize that once you take that step it's 'for richer or for poorer, in sickness and in health, for better or for worse, till death us do part.'" This kind of commitment can give you what you need in order to survive the difficulties. On the other hand, if you know that there is an easy way out, you won't bother to try.

Our society does not recognize marriage as a divine institution and is not committed to it. But when the wedding vows include a deep commitment, a couple can build on that commitment a superstructure of thoroughly mature living.

One of the most beautiful things about marriage is to observe couples who have truly committed themselves to that relationship. Believe it or not, love can grow! I know couples who have been married forty, fifty, and even sixty years. One spouse may be nursing the other, but their love is growing more Christlike as they serve one another. Josh McDowell and Paul Lewis wrote a book called *Givers, Takers and Other Kinds of Lovers*. It's the givers who are truly lovers!

Marriage Creates a Unique Entity

After talking about "leaving" and "cleaving" (v. 7), Jesus also says, "The two will become one flesh. . . . They are no longer two, but one. Therefore, what God has joined together, let man not separate" (vv. 8-9). Thus, when two people marry, they become a unique entity. God has a special kind of mathematics. He can make one plus one equal one.

During a marriage ceremony in our church, we often have the man enter the sanctuary, with all his support group, through one door near the front. (It's astonishing how many people a fellow needs at that particular moment!) I always give the group a little pep talk before they come in; then they enter, looking very stiff in their rented tuxedos. Down the aisle come all the ladies, and finally, at the end of this procession, the bride comes in on her father's arm. The groom takes one position, and the bride another. He's one and she's one.

They stand before the world, one and one. I have done dozens upon dozens of weddings, and I never do one without a sense of awe because I know something very remarkable is going to happen. The officiating minister leads them into something very remarkable. After that age-old rite is performed, God joins them together. The couple goes out a totally new entity. God has joined them together.

Marriage is analogous to the creation of water by combining hydrogen and oxygen (colorless, odorless gases) and passing an electrical charge through them. In fusing these two substances, a totally new entity is created. The new entity is made exclusively of the other two, but it far exceeds the sum of the parts of the two.

In the same way, when God unites the bride and groom, he takes all their qualities and fuses them into a new entity. He takes the best and the worst, the strengths and weaknesses of both, and fuses them into each other so that they might be mutually complementary and enriching. As we begin to understand this, we also begin to see the very real possibilities of marriage.

Have you noticed how opposites attract—for about six weeks? After that opposites irritate. Wouldn't you think that when God in his wisdom brings two people together, they would be people who could agree on the temperature of the house? Wouldn't you think that when God ordains two people from eternity to be made for each other, they would be people who had been brought up to treat toothpaste in the same way?

If we have come to recognize that two have become one, we also have begun to see that these two are melded into a new oneness. But this process requires adjustment and commitment. Why do marriages fail? Because people are not prepared to accept that marriage is a divine institution and refuse to recognize the divine principle of sexuality.

Jesus goes back to the beginning when he says that man and wife are no longer two but one flesh. This is a clear statement concerning the physical aspect of the union. One flesh. In essence, this means that in a complete marriage, there is a coming together in every aspect of life that is demonstrated in the physical union of two people in sexual intercourse. In a marriage where there is not a healthy sexual union, something is profoundly lacking. But by the same token, when people have sexual relations outside of the oneness of marriage that only God can create, theirs is just an imitation of a true "one-flesh" relationship.

The sexual act is intended to demonstrate that as two people surrender and fuse their bodies, they have surrendered and fused themselves—for richer, for poorer, in sickness, in health, till death do them part. And God has sealed it. The sexual act demonstrates this in a unique and beautiful way. Outside the marital relationship, sexual intercourse has no reality behind it. The subjects are not committed to each other, nor has God joined them. Their oneness is a lie, a sham.

Marriage Works by God's Design, Not Ours

We have certainly never lacked for advice on what it means to be a husband or a wife. Many people are more than happy to make sure we are in our correct places, playing the right roles. Unfortunately, these roles, as society has ordained them, have always carried with them gross inequities and brazen inconsistencies with Scripture. Paul challenged his contemporaries to correct the inequities between husbands and wives, between parents and children, and between slaveholders and slaves. He contended that people are holy and distinct only as they practice the principle of mutual submission in these relationships. Let's take a closer look at this situation in Paul's day as it related to marriage.

Marriages in the Greek world were disastrous for women. In *The Complete Woman*, Patricia Gundry explains that the "great men" of that day did not need wives for sexual fulfillment, love, or companionship. The temple prostitutes, who were superbly skillful in all kinds of erotic behavior, often satisfied the sexual needs of these men. In terms of love, many of the noble men believed that true love could exist only between men, so homosexuality was rampant in Greek culture. Companionship was provided by lady entertainers who were skilled in music and discussion.

In contrast, the Greek husband looked upon his wife as merely a fertile field. Just as a farmer sowed his seed in a fertile field to produce a crop, so did the Greek husband plant his seed in his wife to reproduce his kind. In modern vernacular, the Greek wife was a baby machine. In conjunction with this, it was customary for Greek girls to marry as young as fourteen years of age, while the men often waited until they were thirty or thirty-five to marry.

In addressing that inequitable situation, the apostle Paul said, in effect: "Come on, you Christians, those of you who have come out of Greek society; show us that you are holy and distinctive. Forsake this gross perversion of marriage and begin to submit to one another. Make this the basis of a loving, caring relationship in the power of the Holy Spirit."

In many ways, the Hebrew concept of marriage and women was

not that different. Women were also regarded as fertile fields. They were not allowed to be in certain places. As was mentioned previously, to appear in public with their hair hanging loose or uncovered was considered particularly seductive.

Why was woman considered so seductive? Well, she came from Eve, didn't she? Eve had been seduced and was therefore susceptible to all kinds of seduction—women were just that way. Apparently these proper Jewish men forgot that, according to Scripture, the woman was deceived, but Adam went in with his eyes wide open. In Jewish thinking, women were blamed for everything.

Jewish women were regarded as morally and intellectually inferior to men and could not be witnesses in a court of law. Why? The men reasoned that all women were liars, because Sarah had been a liar. Sarah did lie, you recall, when she claimed to be her husband's sister. But she did this on the advice of her husband, Abraham. That, of course, was irrelevant to Jewish men: Sarah was a liar, but Abraham was okay. This exemplifies the kind of unfair thinking and inequity between the sexes that existed among the Jews of that day.

The same inequity prevails today in Moslem courts of law. Some years ago when my wife and I were in Nigeria, we attended a trial with a friend. The entire courtroom suddenly rang with laughter at one point, and we were quite puzzled by it. Our friend then explained that when a lady had stood to give her testimony, all the men in the room began to laugh. Then the judge himself started to laugh, banging his fist on the desk, doubling over with merriment. "What on earth is going on?" I asked. According to my friend, the judge had just reminded the woman that it takes the testimony of one hundred women to equal the testimony of one man. That's the way it is in Islamic Nigeria.

We have already noted Paul's challenge to this type of inequality between men and women, particularly in marriage. In essence, his appeal to the men of his day was: "Gentlemen, let's be different. Let's be distinctive. Let's establish marriages characterized by love in the power of the Holy Spirit—marriages that are lived out in the light. Let's show this crazy society of ours what it is really like for a man and woman to live before the Lord in the fullness of his will for us."

We need to see marriages like this today. We do not necessarily resemble the Greeks or Jews or Romans in marriage, but so many modern marriages are in trouble that there needs to be a revolutionary, radical change in our normal practices. Rather than being adversaries, husbands and wives need to support one another.

Real Marriages Are Partnerships

In Ephesians 5:23 Paul writes, "The husband is the head of the wife as Christ is the head of the church, his body, of which he is the Savior. Now as the church submits to Christ, so also wives should submit to their husbands in everything." In contemporary usage, *head* means "boss." We think of a headmaster, the one in control. But is this a valid way of interpreting what Paul meant in this verse?

Ephesians 4:15-16 reads, "Speaking the truth in love, we will in all things grow up into him who is the Head, that is, Christ. From him the whole body, joined and held together by every supporting ligament, grows and builds itself up in love, as each part does its work" (NIV).

What do these verses suggest? First, the head provides the whole body with sustenance for growing and building up itself in love. The head is the source of life and blessing to the body. Second, in verse 16 the head is described as the integrating factor that joins the body together.

In Ephesians 5, the head is variously referred to as the Savior of the body, the Lord of the church, and the lover of the bride. So if we are going to think in terms of headship (a word not found in the Bible), we must be careful not to simplify it to mean "boss" or "one in control." While the idea of authority is inherent in this word, it goes far beyond that basic concept.

What does it mean for the husband who is seeking to be the head of the wife? He must radically change his view of what it means to be head, for according to Paul's teaching, headship involves servanthood. The husband's role is to be all that God wants him to be as provider for and encourager to his wife. If men fulfilled that role, 90 percent of the marital problems in our society would be solved.

The world needs husbands with radically changed perspectives on marriage. Their philosophy must be not *What can I get?* but *What can I give?* They must accept the privilege of being a source of life and blessing to their wives. Instead of being authoritative and dictatorial, they must be loving and caring.

In 1 Peter 3:7 we read: "Husbands, in the same way be considerate as you live with your wives, and treat them with respect as . . . heirs with you of the gracious gift of life." This revolutionary teaching by Peter—that women were equally heirs of the grace of life—amazed the men of that time. For in Peter and Paul's day, men were the legal heirs of life. They strutted around and had everything going their way. The women entertained them, met their sexual needs, managed their homes, and produced sons (and heirs). Women were locked into roles determined by the men.

Husbands, do you look at your wives from Peter's perspective? Are you as concerned about their spiritual fulfillment as you are about your own? Do you treat them with genuine respect?

Many of us men are extremely gifted at being inconsiderate. We fail to see the deep hurts and intense fears of our wives. We are notoriously insensitive—and the people we live with have the scars to prove it. It seems to be a characteristic of the male ego. Peter is telling us that because women are coheirs with men of "the gracious gift of life," they are equally citizens of the kingdom of heaven.

Marriage Imposes a Profound Responsibility

Jesus' final words to the Pharisees in Mark 10:1-9 are, "Therefore what God has joined together, let man not separate" (NIV). If God created marriage, we should do absolutely nothing to destroy it. This is a profound responsibility. Is there a real possibility that our actions could break up a marriage? God has said, in such a case, the union we are breaking up is something he has put together.

Consider some questions with me. First, are we allowing our marriage to collapse by default because we refuse to work on it, to make adjustments, to build in what is necessary? Remember that God joined couples together so they could discover his plan for them—a new and divine oneness. If by default we allow it to collapse, one day God will ask, "Why did you let my creation collapse?"

Second, are we guilty of being too casual about our sexuality? Are we abusing that divine spark within us? Are we carelessly toying with an alternative lifestyle, feeling that we can do it without bringing on ourselves any bad effects? Remember this: God ordained marriage; and if we are doing anything to smudge that divine principle, we will answer for it.

Third, consider the Old English expression "Marry in haste; repent at leisure." We have to live with our bad choices, so a hasty decision can mean a lifetime of misery. Bad marriages happen, but we make our own choices. If God has allowed us to marry under these circumstances, he can give us grace to live it through. The far wiser thing, however, is to be very selective in our choice of a mate. Take time—and let God lead. Be absolutely certain that the marriage is made in heaven!

Here's a final thought for those of you who are looking back on a failed marriage. If you are responsible for a broken marriage or feel you are guilty of some unmentionable act, there is forgiveness available. But how do you obtain it? Admit your sin. Repent of it. Don't blame it on anybody else. Call it what it is. Seek God's cleansing and forgiveness, and allow him to gather the broken pieces of your life and put them back together.

What are real marriages made of? Real marriages are made of two people coming together under God, doing it God's way.

Let's Get Practical

1. How is marriage a divine institution?

2. How does marriage benefit us psychologically, socially, and theologically?

3. Who created sex, and for what purposes? How have these purposes been thwarted by our treatment of sex?

4. What is distinctive about the marital commitment described in Scripture? Which popular attitudes about relationships does this type of commitment challenge?

5. How is God's design for marriage different from society's?

6. What makes a marriage a true partnership?

4

Do Real Parents Ever Succeed?

The Bible doesn't say much about parenting. It does explain the fatherhood of God and the sonship of Jesus Christ, so in that way it does set forth guidelines to meaningful family living. But perhaps Deuteronomy 6 is the most helpful passage in providing parents with some specific principles:

These are the commands, decrees and laws the LORD your God directed me to teach you to observe in the land that you are crossing the Jordan to possess, so that you, your children and their children after them may fear the LORD your God as long as you live by keeping all his decrees and commands that I give you, and so that you may enjoy long life. . . . Hear, O Israel: The LORD our God, the LORD is one. Love the LORD your God with all your heart and with all your soul and with all your strength. These commandments that I give you today are to be upon your hearts. Impress them on your children. Talk about them when you sit at home and when you walk along the road, when you lie down and when you get up. . . . In the future, when your son asks you, "What is the meaning of the stipulations, decrees and laws the LORD our God has commanded you?" tell him: "We were slaves of Pharaoh in Egypt, but the LORD brought us out of Egypt with a mighty hand. . . . The LORD commanded us to obey all these decrees and to fear the LORD our God, so that we might always prosper and be kept alive, as is the case today. And if we are careful to obey all this law before the LORD our God, as he has commanded us, that will be our righteousness." (Deuteronomy 6:1-2, 4-7, 20-21, 24-25, NIV)

I meet many parents who seem to be on a real guilt trip. All they ever hear is how poorly they are doing as parents—everything that they're doing wrong. When our young people go to high school, many of them take Psych 1, and then they come home and tell us that the main thing they have learned in the course is what we, their parents, have done wrong. In addition to this, we parents are constantly reminded that our children are what they are because of the impact of certain factors on their lives. For example, their genetic makeup, given to them through no fault of their own, determined the kind of people they became. This doesn't do much to alleviate parental guilt. We hear parents saying, "Our children grew up like that because we gave them our genes. It's our fault." The emphasis of this viewpoint is on *nature*.

Another explanation stresses *nurture:* "We are the people we are because of the environment in which we were brought up. And we provided and produced our kids' environment. So we are responsible for their being such weirdos!"

Obviously, both genes and environment have something to do with the type of people we become. And both factors leave parents feeling guilty. They say, "We put our children in that environment, and we are responsible for bringing them into this situation. It's our fault." Some of this is justified, but much of it is not.

In the rest of this chapter we will consider parents from the standpoint of their success in being effective persons before the Lord, being providers, and being "perfect" in parenting.

Parents Must Succeed As Persons

Deuteronomy 6 points out a very important principle: Before we worry about succeeding as parents, we need to be concerned with succeeding as persons.

I once had an interesting conversation with a mother and her young teenager, who were having some difficulties in their relationship. In the course of our conversation a question came up about the difference between a Christian psychologist and a secular psychologist.

"As far as psychology is concerned," I explained, "there probably is not much difference. Both are trying to make discoveries about human behavior and development. But the Christian psychologist will look at his or her discoveries from a different perspective than will the non-Christian."

How will the Christian psychologist look at it differently?" the young man asked.

"Well," I replied, "if I believe that God created me for a purpose, that God loved me enough to send his Son to die for me, and that I will live in eternity, these beliefs will affect the way I look at myself and at other people. So a Christian psychologist will apply his or her psychological knowledge of clients in terms of their creation, redemption, and eternal significance. Each person will be seen as having a divine purpose that must be discovered. On the other hand, a person who does not apply psychological knowledge from a Christian base will not incorporate all of these factors in his or her thinking."

Principles of Christian parenting

Deuteronomy 6 and the Christian psychologist are alike in that both look at humanity from the divine perspective. Deuteronomy is primarily concerned with the behavior of parents as people before the Lord, not parenting in and of itself. It spells out six principles of behavior for parents to follow: Listen to the Lord (verses 3-4), obey the Lord (verse 3), love the Lord (verse 5), fear the Lord (verse 13), serve the Lord (verse 13), and trust the Lord (verses 18-19).

If we as parents believe we are created by God for a purpose, we need to be concerned about the principles we are building into our lives. We must examine ourselves according to these principles:

Do we spend time listening to the Lord God? Are we eager to live in obedience to him? Do we show him that we love him with all our heart, soul, and strength, so that every day of the week (not just an hour on Sunday), and in all the circumstances of our lives, our love for the Lord is paramount?

In addition, are we honoring the Lord God in all that we do? Whatever we do, is it done "heartily as unto the Lord?"

Are we truly servants of God, or are we the servants of popularity, money, comfort, or some ideology? What, or who, are we serving?

Finally, do we truly trust the Lord? Do we do what we are required to do and then place it before the Lord, trusting him to work it out?

As we begin to live by the principles posed in these questions, we will begin to succeed as persons and also as parents. Our children will begin to observe and learn from our lives—the most fundamental transaction of the parenting experience.

Practicalities of Christian parenting

We must have more going for us than good principles, however. As authentic persons we must also translate those principles into practical relationships within the family. First let's consider the relationship between the parents.

It takes two parents to make a child; ideally, it will also take two parents to raise a child. I am deeply aware that for single parents this will not be possible. In connection with this, I stress that I am addressing what is the scriptural *ideal,* fully recognizing that all of us are sinners, fallen people. We have created a fallen society, and inhabit a fallen environment—hardly a way to live in the ideal. This does not mean, however, that we should not teach the ideal, for we at least know what we are aiming at. While I don't want to add to the burden of single parents, neither do I want to neglect the teaching of God's ideal way.

Parents' relationship with each other. Parents need to translate the principles of living into their relationship with each other. How does this apply to bringing up a child? Why is it important? Children are experts at observing how Mom and Dad interact. And as they observe, they learn important lessons about relationships, and soon they begin to mimic and demonstrate what they are learning.

When our children were very small, Jill called me over to the kitchen window one day. "Would you listen to this?" she said. We looked outside at our three little ones playing in the garden. Judy was standing there, and in front of her were her two brothers, looking very shamefaced. With her hands on her hips, she was saying, "How many times do I have to tell you? I told you, and I told you, and I told you until I am sick of telling you!"

Jill said, "Do you recognize what's going on there?" Judy was a miniature Jill scolding those two little boys.

Children mimic parental behavior because they have no other way to learn during those early years. They are absolute experts at seeing rifts develop between parents, and they can drive a wedge where there is no room for a wedge. How do they do it? They know which parent will say yes and which will say no. So if they want to do something, they avoid the "no" parent. They will then set one parent against the other. And before the parents realize it, the little rascals have created division and discord between them.

How do parents handle this problem? They make absolutely certain that they are unified on their principles of operation as parents. They adhere to those principles in their relationship and thereby convey those beliefs to their children. Children know what parents really believe—by seeing how parents behave.

Parents' relationship with their children. We should also consider the importance of relationships with our children. We need to translate the principles found in Deuteronomy 6 into the parent-child relationship. If we believe that God created us, we have no choice but to believe that the little person who was born into our home is not just a toy to play with, something for our own fulfillment. That little child is a divinely created, eternally significant, profoundly important *person*. If we believe that, we will then translate it into the relationship with the child.

Notice Deuteronomy 6:20, where the son asks the father what is the meaning of the decrees and laws. The father answers his question and says, "If we are careful to obey all this law before the Lord our God, . . . that will be our righteousness" (6:25). This father is saying that righteousness should be our primary concern in life.

Have you ever asked yourself, *What am I trying to do with my life?* Try to put your answer into a paragraph, then into a sentence, and later try to condense it to one word. One of the best phrases you could use to summarize your life would be "a concern for righteousness"—to live rightly before God.

To live rightly before God has all kinds of ramifications, not the least of which is this: If I live rightly before God, I do so in the context of relationships. This means that one aspect of living rightly before God is to treat people rightly, especially those nearest to me. If I'm to succeed as a person, I need to apply the principles of righteousness to every relationship, especially with my mate and my children.

Parents Must Succeed As Providers

We could use many terms to describe what parents do, but I choose to use the word *provider* because it is inclusive. Paul, writing to Timothy, said:

> If anyone does not provide for his relatives, and especially for his immediate family, he has denied the faith and is worse than an unbeliever. (1 Tim. 5:8, NIV)

How could he state his case more emphatically than this? In 2 Corinthians 12:14 (NIV) he writes from another perspective:

> I will not be a burden to you, because what I want is not your possessions but you. After all, children should not have to save up for their parents, but parents for their children.

It is the responsibility of the parents to provide for the children.

That is a simple, fundamental rule.

Let me suggest four areas in which parents must provide for their children: protection, direction, inspection, and correction.

Protection

The human infant is unbelievably dependent—he or she needs a whole year to learn to walk. Compare this to the little foal. Within minutes after birth, it is walking around on wobbly legs. And in a few days, this little horse is running around the pasture. Human children, however, remain helpless for months and require all kinds of protection.

Why do children need this protection? Children need it in order to be healthy, happy, and human. For example, we try not to expose babies to a lot of nasty germs. It becomes problematic, however, when we unduly coddle our little ones. Sometimes I tell my congregation: "Let me say a word to some of you young moms who are so concerned about your little ones that you won't even put them in our nursery: Put them in the nursery. We haven't lost one yet!" Another problem arises when, in our extreme concern with keeping the little ones happy, we spoil them rotten. And ultimately, if we become too preoccupied with keeping them healthy and happy, we may end up with children who are less than civilized and reasonable.

I attended a Milwaukee Brewers game one afternoon and didn't enjoy it for two reasons. One, it was a rotten game. Two, the kid sitting across the aisle from me was a menace. I wanted to minister to that child! Eventually the fellow sitting behind him leaned over, tapped him on the shoulder, and said, "How old are you, son?"

"Seven," the boy replied.

"Would you like to see eight?" the man asked. I doubted very much whether the boy would see eight, because his response was to throw a handful of popcorn in the man's face. And his parents just sat there, saying, "No . . . no . . . no." That was all. The boy was hopelessly out of control. He needed help in becoming a civilized and reasonable human.

Direction

We also need to provide moral and spiritual direction for our children. If we don't do it at home, it is unlikely that they will get any direction. They certainly will not get it in the school system. And I understand why.

The Governor of Wisconsin invites guests to lunch at the executive mansion each month, and one day I was invited as a representative from the religious community. During lunch there developed a free-flowing discussion among those present from the different sectors—business, entertainment, religion, and government. We began to converse about education. Someone asked me, "How do you feel about our educational system?" I replied that I would like to see more values taught. The gentleman seated across from me was a regent from the University of Wisconsin. His expression changed immediately. "Whose values do you want taught, yours or mine?" he said, bristling. He was assuming that our values were different, even though he didn't know mine. When I replied, "Both," he was nonplused. He thought I was going to say "mine!"

What have we done in refusing to teach values in our public school system? We have ended up teaching the value of no values. That is why parents must teach values in the home.

In Deuteronomy 6, the Israelites were told to impress the Lord's commandments upon their children (v. 7). It is all too easy in these times to ignore our responsibility to give moral and spiritual direction to our children. We want to shift the responsibility to other people. But who, besides us, is going to teach our children biblical, spiritual values? Certainly not the educational system, because that system is striving more and more for a "value-neutral" approach in its attempt not to offend anyone.

Neither can we expect our children to derive spiritual values from the media. I am not suggesting that we "pull the plug" or ban all non-Christian movies, music, and books. I do suggest, however, that we pay close attention to what our children are learning. We need to help them evaluate their learning so that it includes fundamental moral and spiritual principles. In line with this, Deuteronomy tells us to talk about these principles when we sit at home, when we walk along the road, when we lie down, and when we get up. We are to tie them as symbols on our hands, bind them on our foreheads, and write them on the door frames of our houses and on our gates (vv. 7-9).

What is the Lord saying here? "Be natural about it." Be perfectly natural about teaching moral and spiritual principles. Do it in the course of everyday living, in a consistent way. Do it in a practical way, but make sure you do it!

In our church, people sometimes say that our youth group has failed to influence their kids. That is quite possible. Look at the youth group in any church. How much contact does the church have with them? Some of the children in Sunday school and Christian education don't have a consistent experience there, because parents are not regularly putting them there. The family often leaves for the weekend, and the kids soon learn that Sunday school and church are not very important. If we expect our kids to gain spiritual training in Sunday school, we must remember that, at best, they are going to get one or two hours a week, and even that isn't consistent in many cases.

What happens as our children grow older? Other activities (school and social) are allowed to take precedence. Too often, our teenagers are not involved in any significant spiritual training. If we are going to work realistically with these kids, we must take responsibility for their moral and spiritual upbringing. We must carefully evaluate what they are learning at school and through the media. We must assure them of adequate spiritual training in the church and the home. This is how we provide direction for them.

Church attendance often becomes a real conflict with older children. The time to settle that problem is when the children are small. From the very beginning, our kids were taught that Sunday was the Lord's day and that our family went to church on Sunday morning and evening. The matter was not negotiable.

Moreover, our children were expected to be involved in a Christian youth activity during the week. We gave them clear direction but allowed some flexibility. They could participate in the youth activity of their choice. It was very interesting to notice that each child chose a different activity.

As our children grew older, we told them that Sunday evening was negotiable. That is, if they had a very good reason not to be in church, we would discuss it, and I would decide. I didn't have any problem with that. If parents are going to be parents, they have to be in charge—not in a dictatorial sense, but in a firm, honest way. We soon discovered that homework was not a valid reason to skip church Sunday evening. We quoted the verse, "Six days shalt thou labor, and do all thy work" (Exod. 20:9, KJV). We decided that children who were out having all kinds of fun and simply leaving their homework until the last minute on Sunday needed more direction than they were getting.

When the Super Bowl was switched to a Sunday, I knew what was going through my youngest son's mind. As I was getting ready to go to church, I said, "Pete, do you know what is on television tonight?"

He replied, "Yes, the Super Bowl."

"Do you feel that the Super Bowl is a high priority in your life?" I asked.

He said, "Yes, I do."

"Probably most of the people at Elmbrook also regard it as a high priority," I said. "I'll be perfectly frank with you. I would like to see it too. Unfortunately, I can't, but do you think you could make a good case for not going to church tonight and for watching the Super Bowl instead?"

"Oh," he said, "I think I could make a marvelous case for it."

And he did! He totally convinced me that he ought to stay home and watch the Super Bowl. For me it was a case of principle with built-in flexibility.

Some people have asked me, "What about family devotions?" In our family, our initial efforts at family devotions were a disaster. We soon discovered that it was practically impossible in our household to get everyone together at a specific time for devotions. In the end we chose a very simple solution. If we couldn't have devotions together, we would teach our kids to have devotions on their own, and we would supervise them. So, rather early in their lives, our kids began to develop their own personal style of devotions. It was interesting to observe their different styles. When Dave, our eldest, was in high school, he would come home from school, run three to five miles cross-country, and go straight up to his room for half an hour. Sometimes he would get so irate because of the noise in the house that he would open the door and yell, "Be quiet; I'm having my devotions!"

One day I picked up a Bible, thinking it was mine, but it was Dave's. I opened it to one of the Epistles and couldn't believe what I saw. He had written out each of the Epistles in his own language between the lines of print. Nobody told him to. It was something he figured out and did on his own.

You may not be able to have family devotions, but if you can—great! Do it as long as you can. But don't make it a battleground or such a stressful issue that everyone ends up hating the exercise. Experiment and try to find the best ways to do it. If you can't do it together, do it separately. But make sure that you are giving your children this sense of direction.

What about direction for everyday matters, and for socializing? Parents provide this for their kids by what they say and do. Recently I heard about a young wife who was going to boil a ham for a special event. In preparing it, she cut off both ends. Her husband watched her and asked, "Why did you cut off both ends of that ham? You waste a lot of meat."

"You always do it that way," she replied.

"I never heard of anyone doing it that way," he said.

She went on, "My mother always did it that way."

Shortly thereafter, they went to a celebration at her mother's house. Sure enough they had ham, and wouldn't you know it—both ends of the ham were cut off.

The young son-in-law then went to his mother-in-law and asked, "Tell me, why do you cut off both ends of the ham?"

She replied, "Oh, my mother always did it that way."

So the young husband approached the grandmother and said, "Excuse me, but when you boil a ham, do you cut off both ends of the ham?"

She replied, "Yes, I always do."

He asked, "Why?"

She answered, "The pan isn't big enough." So you see, parents' ways affect their children's ways of doing things! Parents must remember that—consciously or unconsciously—they are giving direction to their children, and that we always run the risk of giving them the *wrong* direction. The wise writer of Proverbs said, "Train a child in the way he should go, and when he is old he will not turn from it" (22:6). The problem is figuring out which way he should go. Some people say that a child should be allowed to go his own way. "I don't interfere with my kids," they say. "I just let them go the way they want to go." Proverbs also has a word for them: "A child left to himself disgraces his mother" (29:15). Parents must walk a fine line between letting their children do whatever pleases them and being so strict that they are thwarted from developing into the unique persons God wants them to be.

How do we find out what it is our children should do? We must be sensitive to each young person's God-given potential. "The way that he or she should go" must be aligned with God's "should."

Let me put it another way. Do you remember how ships used to go to sea under sealed orders in wartime? The commander didn't know his destination until he was two or three days out to sea—then he would open his sealed orders to find out. When a child comes into the world, he or she has sealed orders. Part of the parenting process is to help children discover their destiny, their sealed orders. It is not our duty as parents to impose our desires upon our children, or to force them into our mold. *Rather, our job is to assist our children in discovering what God wants them to do with their lives.* Children need direction, not coercion.

Inspection

Inspection is the third provision parents must make for their children. A child needs this kind of attention, because he will bring shame to his mother if left to himself. This is a disservice to the child.

I examined our vegetable garden the other day. It was full of gorgeous yellow flowers called broccoli, a green vegetable of the mustard family. If you cut off the head before it flowers, the plant keeps on growing; you may find yourself eating broccoli until you never want to see another broccoli dish. I've found a way to cure that problem—just leave the plant untended and unpruned, and it will produce gorgeous yellow flowers. As I continued to look at the garden, I felt somewhat ashamed. In the same way that a garden left to itself will simply go to seed, a child left to himself will miss important cultivation and care that would have produced the character God intended. Children and gardens are similar in that they go to seed very quickly. So we need to keep a keen eye on children and inspect what they are doing.

But we must take care. Inspection does not mean that we invade our children's privacy. For example, when daughters start getting letters from some mysterious source, mothers must resist the temptation to steam the envelope open. We learned one thing very quickly in relating to our children: As soon as they were old enough to be alone (and we had a home that was big enough), they were given a room, a place to call their own. And we had a very simple rule: When they went into that room and closed the door, we knocked before we entered. That was their little island of privacy—we respected them as persons. This did not mean that they were left to themselves to do their own thing. It did mean that there was careful supervision and inspection of what they were doing.

When our daughter Judy began to go out with her girl friends, they would talk on the phone constantly. One day some of her friends came over so that they could attend a movie together. As they were rushing out the door, I said to Judy, "What movie are you going to see?" She told me.

I asked, "What is the rating?"

"PG."

"What does that mean? Pretty good?"

"No," she said, "it means parental guidance."

"Really? Which parent gave you guidance on it?"

"Oh," she said, "Daddy, it's just . . . I've got to go."

"I understand you've got to go, but which parent gave you guidance on this movie?" I went on. "You said it was PG; I didn't."

"Come on Daddy, you're embarrassing me."

"Judy," I said, "you really need to get parental guidance on these things."

"I know it. There is only one bad part in this movie."

"I know, Judy. It's at the beginning, and you've already missed it. You can go now!"

It does help to know what movies your children are seeing. If you can't screen them yourself, don't plan to go with your kids— that would embarrass them no end! Instead, talk with them about the matter at an appropriate time. Decide with them what they can and can't see. If you have children in your home and don't have cable TV, think it over carefully before you subscribe. Then think it over again!

Correction

Finally, parents must provide their children with correction. Proverbs 22:15 tells us that "folly is bound up in the heart of a child, but the rod of discipline will drive it far from him."

When we correct our children, we must make the punishment fit the crime, which is sometimes difficult. My parents wore out a cane on me, and to add insult to injury, they made me buy a new one out of my pocket money. I do suggest that we maintain control of ourselves and that we never punish our children when we're angry. We also need to explain the disciplinary situation to them and provide them with plenty of opportunity to ask questions.

In our family, we learned to discipline each child differently. Initially, I would spank our son Dave until my hand hurt, but he wouldn't cry or change his mind. He would just look at me with those big brown eyes, as if to say, "You're a real dummy, aren't you?" But I did find that denying him certain simple privileges would totally mortify him. That was the only way to control him.

As far as Judy was concerned, we didn't have to spank her or deny her any privileges. We only had to look at her and say, "Judy!" She was so easy to handle that I felt guilty about it at times. Our third one was raised by the other two—or so they say!

How do you maintain control of your children as they grow older? We have discovered that it can be relatively easy to maintain control of your children if you maintain control of their money.

I know many parents who believe that their kids ought to work. They point out how they grew up on a farm and learned to work there. I can't believe how many people grew up on farms. There must have been one hundred fifty kids on every farm in Wisconsin! You know how it goes: "I grew up on a farm and was up milking the cows at 4:30 in the morning." That makes quite a story.

There's a flip side to this idea of children working. If your kids make all kinds of money, fine. If your kids then put all kinds of money into their own bank accounts—it's not so fine. You've lost control. It will only be a matter of time before they buy "wheels." When they have their own bank account and their own wheels, you've lost them.

Why do parents have to maintain control? Because children must learn authority, discipline, and responsibility, and this requires inspection and correction by their parents. If parents don't have the means to inspect and correct their children, it is highly possible that they won't be able to teach them. For that reason I strongly advise parents not to surrender economic control of their kids while they are at home and still teenagers.

It is better to relinquish control gradually and give your children more and more freedom and independence. And if you are going to provide correction, you need to be sure that you have the means to do so.

Are Parents Succeeding at Perfection?

Why do we think that we have to be perfect parents when we are not perfect at anything else? We must remember that when we have done our best as parents, our children still have minds of their own, and they will make their own decisions. Our best effort will be to give them a foundation for making good decisions. We must let them learn to make their own decisions, which will be horrifying and disastrous sometimes. But all of these experiences are part of the growing-up process, for parents as well as for children.

I have some words of encouragement for you at this point:

Hear, O heavens! Listen, O earth!
For the LORD has spoken:
"I reared children and brought them up,
but they have rebelled against me." (Isaiah 1:2, NIV)

If any people had a good upbringing, it was the children of Israel. Jehovah himself raised them. But when they came to the age of decision, they rebelled against him. So we can't accept total responsibility for the way our kids turn out, because they have minds of their own.

However, parents must beware of having unrealistic expectations of their children. Paul has something to say to us here: "Fathers, do not exasperate your children; instead, bring them up in the training and instruction of the Lord" (Eph. 6:4, NIV).

Neither should parents exert excessive pressure on their children. Paul tells the Colossians, "Fathers, do not embitter your children, or they will become discouraged" (3:21, NIV). Parents must not abuse their privileged position by frustrating their kids unnecessarily. The Bible has been careful to reiterate this principle: Be very careful, parents, not to pressure your children unduly. Parents often do this by making unfair demands and then being inconsistent themselves.

Sometimes parents expect more from their children than they deliver in terms of their own lifestyle. Some years ago, when I was flying from Jamaica to New York, a little lady beside me chain-smoked the entire trip. She was literally lighting one cigarette off the other.

I asked her, "Are you nervous?"

Her reply was, "I am very nervous."

"Why?"

"I have twin daughters at home, and I've left them for the week. I'm just nervous about what they are up to."

I asked, "Do you have reason to worry about them?"

"Yes, I do. I just know they will be smoking pot."

"I imagine that they are," I said. "I would be surprised if they weren't."

Here she was, down on her daughters for smoking pot. I continued: "I know what they are going to tell you: 'Hey, Mother, you smoke tobacco, and the nicotine in it has been proven to be addictive. We smoke marijuana, which [at that time] has not been proven to be addictive. Who is smart? You or us?' "

We shouldn't get nervous about our kids smoking pot if we are smoking the other stuff. We should not worry about our kids drinking if we are showing them how to drink. We cannot demand of them what we do not demand of ourselves.

In conclusion, we must not ignore the failures of our children. If we know that our kids are seriously misbehaving, we must try to lead them to repentance. But we must do it with compassion and in a spirit of forgiveness. We must correct them in love, not bitterness. And we must not forget to intercede and seek divine intervention in their behalf. Without God in our boat, we'll sink for sure; with him at our side, all things are possible in this business of parenting.

Do real parents ever succeed? The answer is yes, but the path to success is not an easy one. The old prayer proverb fits this whole task of parenting: "Pray as if everything depended on God, and work as if everything depended on you." That's the secret to parenting with power.

Let's Get Practical

1. List some principles from Deuteronomy 6 that can assist us in our parenting.

2. In what ways do parents provide the following for their children?

    protection:

    direction:

    inspection:

    correction:

3. What aspects of parenting are most difficult for you? List some ideas for getting help in these areas.

4. How can you, as a parent, gain encouragement from God's Word? Which passages or stories have been most helpful to you in the past?

5

Teenagers in Search of Genuine Life

The term *teenager* is not found in the Bible, but that doesn't mean it ignores the subject. For example, we know of a very significant event in Jesus' life when he was twelve years of age—that's pretty close to the teen years. Luke's account of this particular episode gives us some insight into the experience of young people during these years.

Every year [Jesus'] parents went to Jerusalem for the Feast of the Passover. When he was twelve years old, they went up to the Feast, according to the custom. After the Feast was over, while his parents were returning home, the boy Jesus stayed behind in Jerusalem, but they were unaware of it. Thinking he was in their company, they traveled on for a day. Then they began looking for him among their relatives and friends. When they did not find him, they went back to Jerusalem to look for him. After three days they found him in the temple courts, sitting among the teachers, listening to them and asking them questions. Everyone who heard him was amazed at his understanding and his answers. When his parents saw him, they were astonished. His mother said to him, "Son, why have you treated us like this? Your father and I have been anxiously searching for you."

"Why were you searching for me?" he asked. "Didn't you know I had to be in my Father's house?" But they did not understand what he was saying to them.

Then he went down to Nazareth with them and was obedient to them. But his mother treasured all these things in her heart. And Jesus grew in wisdom and stature, and in favor with God and men. (Luke 2:41-52, NIV)

Adolescence is a common word, but it's not found in the Bible anywhere at all. Although adolescents have always been with us, the term itself is peculiar to the twentieth century. The term literally means the period of growth between childhood and adulthood. Without question, it should not be classified as the easiest period of life.

We sometimes refer to these turbulent years as the "tumultuous teens." Some knowledgeable people think that it is probably more difficult to be an adolescent now than ever before. What can real teenagers do about the challenge of growing from childhood to adulthood through the perilous period called adolescence?

Teenagers are people in process, in that very difficult transition between childhood and adulthood. Treasured aspects of their personality are still childlike (some would even say childish), but in other areas they are surprisingly mature. This uneasy mix of characteristics causes significant difficulty and tension.

They are also people under pressure. Change is inevitable for people in process. When change occurs, some form of trauma is also unavoidable. As we face change, we are moving into the unknown, which always produces some degree of apprehension.

But we must also remember that a teenager is a person of amazing potential. Parents, teachers, and other adults in a teen's life must take care to remind that young man or woman of just how much potential he or she possesses. The possibilities for reaching goals and developing strengths and gifts is enormous.

As we take a closer look at these three aspects of a teenager, we will use the model of the youthful Jesus.

A Person in Process

Luke 2:52 speaks of Jesus being in a transitional stage: "And Jesus grew in wisdom and stature, and in favor with God and men" (NIV). The Greek word for "grew" here means "to progress, to advance, to move." Adolescence is characterized by tremendous progress, movement, and growth.

Luke also points out four aspects of Jesus' growth. He says that Jesus grew "in wisdom" (psychologically), "in stature" (physically), "in favor with God" (spiritually), and "in favor with men" (socially).

Psychological growth

First, Jesus grew "in wisdom," a very important concept in the Old Testament. Proverbs 1:7 (KJV) says, "The fear of the Lord is the beginning of knowledge, but fools despise wisdom and instruction."

Clarence Darrow, well-known debater and attorney of a past generation, said the exact opposite. He believed the fear of the Lord is "the end of wisdom." And he said that God is a figment of a person's imagination and will only retard that person's development and growth. But the Bible says, in effect, if Jesus is Lord of your life, if you give him first place in your life, then your life will begin to make sense.

The New Testament also has something important to say about wisdom. James teaches that wisdom can come from two sources. It can come from above and bring great benefits, or it can come from below and be very destructive in your life (James 3:15-17).

What does wisdom mean? It's more than just learning information, whether it be thrust at us by school teacher, a preacher, or some other source. When we speak of wisdom, we're talking about properly *applied* information. If we begin to apply information, our attitudes will change. And if our attitudes are changed, our activities and our actions will change. Thus, wisdom means getting information, knowing how to apply it, and changing our attitudes and behavior accordingly.

Jesus grew "in wisdom," and so do teenagers. Depending on their source of information and how they apply it, their attitudes and actions will change for the better—or for the worse. James says if you get the wrong information (from below) and apply it to your life, it will affect your attitude, and your actions will identify your source of information. Or, he says, if you get your information from above, it will affect you as you apply it; your attitudes will be changed, and your activities will demonstrate it. This is a tremendous process for the teenager, because he or she is beginning to learn concepts and principles and to discover what it means to act on them.

Let me give you an example. When you were a child, you didn't even know what authority was, but you knew how it felt! It meant that you had to do what your parents said or else. As time went on, you went to school and learned more about authority. From history you learned how it was exercised properly and improperly by the army and by politicians. And you learned that you have to make an important decision: You must choose your own personal attitude toward authority. How will you personally react to the authority of your parents, teachers, and coach? Your attitudes and actions will reveal your progress in growing up.

Physical growth

The Bible says that Jesus grew "in stature." That meant, of course, that he experienced certain bodily changes. Both boys and girls go through tremendous physical changes in their teens. The whole process is traumatic, and while it's often the subject of ridicule and jokes, it's not funny. Physiological changes are most evident in terms of sexuality, skin, and stature. Some young men become "hunks" by their sixteenth birthday, and others are still in the "imp" category by their nineteenth year. It matters deeply to both the "hunk" and the "imp." Some girls blossom in the appropriate places and find ways to display their accomplishments while their less favorably endowed sisters do all that they can to cover their embarrassment and their shortcomings.

A friend of mine says that getting older is traumatic because when he was young all he worried about was pimples and now he's worried about tumors! That's true, but teenagers look at pimples as if they were tumors and would gladly go through surgery if they thought it would help. It helps to remember, however, that Jesus went through these same physical changes; it is all a part of normal growth, and this stage will pass. The fact that we are told that Jesus grew in stature is a reminder that our bodies and what they go through are important—just as growth in wisdom is important.

Spiritual growth

In Luke's words, Jesus "increased in favor with God." Children normally believe basically what their parents believe. If the parents are divided in their beliefs, that makes it particularly tough for the kids. To get along with their parents, they are forced to vacillate between them. The emotional trauma of seesawing back and forth is bound to take its toll and retard their spiritual growth.

As children grow older, their faith (which is born of conformity) begins to be battered by all kinds of challenges. "You say you believe in God," some teacher taunts. "Could God make a stone so big he couldn't move it?" If one says yes, the answer comes, "If he couldn't move it, he is not God!"

"Where did Cain get his wife?" another asks. How do you answer that? These are the kinds of questions confronting our kids.

As children we believed what our parents believed, and there is nothing wrong with that, providing they were telling us the right things. But when our faith comes under scrutiny, the challenge begins. It is important for all of us to think through our faith until it becomes our own. When young people re-examine what they have been taught and accept its validity on a mature level, this is true spiritual growth.

Social growth

Jesus grew "in favor with . . . men." Human beings are social creatures, but the last thing some teenagers want is to be social. Because they are so shy and self-conscious, they would prefer to stand in a corner and watch the world go by. Others really enjoy social activities. Let's face it, however; growing up is a social process—one that is influenced by at least three factors.

One of these factors is the *social structures within our homes.* You and I were born into this world without being consulted. No one discussed the matter with us or asked our permission; nor could we pick our family. Immediately, social structures were built around us, social structures that were chosen by our parents. They gave us our values and imposed their controls upon us. As small children, we didn't even know we could rebel against them; and even when we did find it out, we discovered that these controls were stronger than our rebellion.

If our home was reasonably healthy, the social structures of our parents provided us with a sense of security, because we knew parameters of our behavior. If they told us to come home at a certain time and we disobeyed, certain consequences followed, some of them unpleasant. They mandated the controls, and we learned to live in the resultant social structure. The sense of security in this controlled atmosphere made us feel that we could always go home and be accepted there.

A second factor in social growth is the *presence and attraction of our peers.* During adolescence both the teen and the parent face a disconcerting transition. The teen doesn't want to be seen with Mom or Dad, whether it is walking in a shopping mall, on vacation, or at church. Something else has become more important than Mom and Dad. In spite of their usefulness, they seem quite out of things. Their opinions clash with seemingly "new" information now provided by peers.

There's nothing wrong with this if parents and peers are in total agreement. I've never know this to happen, however, and that's where the problem arises. As we grow up, we want to move away from parental control. We examine our parents' values and become involved in the excitement of our peers. We begin to experiment and to explore other viewpoints and lifestyles.

The third factor in social growth is our *new awareness of the opposite sex*. It is quite normal for little boys and little girls to ignore one another. At times they may become downright antagonistic toward each other—and then the lightning strikes! Something mysterious happens. That gangly little girl next door, who used to sport braces and zits, is blossoming into a beautiful woman. Suddenly the boys begin to take interest. That interest is expressed, awkwardly or shyly. Acceptance or rejection follows. Acceptance means that both teens are walking a mile above the earth, hardly able to think straight. Rejection becomes the most overwhelming hurt imaginable. This is all part of the growing-up process. It's one of the toughest times we face as human beings.

Fortunately, teens are young and resilient. But in big and small ways, they still need the support of Mom and Dad as they make their way through the social jungle. Sometimes Mom and Dad aren't the right people; sometimes the more objective friendship of another adult in the faith community is exactly what a teen needs to get through the ups and downs, the hurts and victories of the ever-changing social scene.

A Person under Pressure

An adolescent is a person under pressure, a natural result of being a person in process. In this pressurized atmosphere the teenager must learn to be wise, to apply knowledge rightly in day-by-day situations, and to learn different ways of behaving.

Let me illustrate. The scene is the local supermarket. A young mother is making her way down one of the aisles, wheeling a toddler in her grocery cart. The little one starts yelling and screaming. She's seen something she wants, and Mother won't let her have it. You've heard of "impulse buying"? It's not the mother's impulse; it's the kid's. It's a kind of blackmail if the mother gives in to the tantrum.

What does the mother say to the child? Chances are she'll say something like, "Act your age!" But that's the problem. The child *is* acting her age. But the mother is finding it difficult to allow her to be that age. So it is with teenagers.

The fact is, children don't grow up overnight. Parents, give your children a chance to grow up. Help them, through your understanding and modeling of the right kind of behavior. Don't be childish in your own actions and then expect your children to act like adults.

Unfortunately, teenagers don't always choose the best models in today's turbulent society; their role models are more often antiheroes rather than positive patterns for behavior. Too often our children admire and emulate entertainers like Prince, Madonna, Mariah Carey, Kurt Cobain, River Phoenix, or Megadeth. Parents need to set a good example for their kids and encourage them to choose wholesome heroes and heroines.

What's it like out there for young people? It's estimated that from grades seven through twelve a typical teenager listens to 10,560 hours of rock music. Teachers may get as many as 7,000 hours of their time. Who do you think has the most impact?

Parents need to know what their children are listening to and offer them viable alternatives and better role models. The magazine *The New Republic* characterized Madonna as an expert at "exuding innocence and decadence." Thirteen-year-old girls worship at her shrine, and they don't even know what she stands for. The innocence and decadence are so subtly shown that adults miss her message altogether. Young people need straightforward sexual information, but they won't get it from Madonna and Prince! Yet they are listening to these voices.

Parents must help their children understand their sexuality. We must recognize and help them cope with the tremendous pressures they are experiencing as they mature both physically and psychologically.

Several years ago two surgeons did research on eleven thousand inmates in prison for serious, violent crimes. They discovered that 60 percent had surgically correctable facial deformities (the figure in the general population is 20 percent). What does this tell us? Violent criminals are three times more likely to have a facial deformity than the general population. The researchers concluded that a primary cause of criminal behavior is the rejection experienced by many adolescents because of their appearance. The way we look, particularly during those traumatic teenage years, is all-important and can have a profound impact upon us.

Life is not easy. Growing up psychologically is hard. But what about growing up spiritually? Inevitably, it seems, spiritual growth requires us to live through a period of doubt. The trouble with doubt is the guilt one feels about having it. It's bad enough to have doubts; to feel guilty about it adds even more internal pressure.

Young people should not be afraid to think about their faith and ask questions. They have to learn that all of their questions will not be answered; in fact, the sooner they learn this the better, because there are some false teachers out there who claim to know all the answers. Spiritual growth cannot be put down in a simple formula, and during insecure periods of life—such as adolescence—we want things to be simple! But the most important thing a teenager can understand is that following after God and seeking fellowship with him is up to us—and the growth is up to God.

Growing up also involves social pressure. As children, we are dependent on our parents; but as we grow older, we seek independence. We cannot remain totally dependent on our parents.

Picture a seventeen-year-old boy walking through a shopping mall, holding his mommy's hand and crying "Mommy, Mommy!" He has a problem—his mother. For some reason, she isn't letting him have the independence he needs, and he isn't demanding it either. The normal process is that we go from dependence to independence to mature interdependence. One of the nice features of this process is that parents can watch their children become adults who in turn become their friends.

A problem arises when some moms and dads don't want to let go of their children, or aren't willing to give them as much freedom as they want. The other extreme can happen as well—some parents can't wait to get rid of their children. We need a balanced approach.

Perfectly normal attempts at independence should not be perceived as rebellion by parents. When does the push for independence become rebellion? It depends on your perspective. In my homeland, England, the Revolutionary War was considered a rebellion, but in the United Sates it is remembered as a battle for independence. When does a terrorist become a freedom fighter? It depends on which side of the ocean you are on. When does a teenager, who normally pushes us to the limit to achieve a little independence, become rebellious? That's a question teachers and parents need to answer. But in doing so, we must always remember that teenagers have every right to some independence and can become downright rebellious when they are pushed too hard.

The Potential of Youth

Even though they are under tremendous pressure from every side, we also need to remember that teenagers have enormous potential. Chapter 12 of Ecclesiastes deals with this issue: "Remember your Creator in the days of your youth, before the days of trouble come and the years approach when you will say, 'I find no pleasure in them' " (v. 1).

In other words, life is made up of changes. As we grow older, we do not function as well physically as we did in our youth. So the time to serve God is now. The book continues to describe old age as a time "when the keepers of the house tremble, and the strong men stoop, when the grinders cease because they are few, and those looking through the windows grow dim . . . when men rise up at the sound of birds; but all their songs grow faint; when men are afraid of heights and of dangers in the streets; when the almond tree blossoms and the grasshopper drags himself along and desire no longer is stirred" (vv. 3-5, NIV).

What is the point of all this? We shouldn't wait until we are old to be what we were created to be. Even though we are young, we are created to be someone and to do something. We need to get on with it, then. "Remember him—before the silver cord is severed, or the golden bowl is broken" (v. 6). In the days when this was written, light was provided by golden bowls of oil suspended on a silver cord. When the silver cord wore thin and broke, the golden bowl would spill and the light would go out. Our lives are like this. While we are young, we have a strong silver cord and a bright shiny bowl, full of vigor and enthusiasm. God can set our bowl alight so that we can do what we were intended to do. We must not wait until the old cord has snapped and all the oil has spilled.

There's another picture in verse 6: "before the pitcher is shattered at the spring." In Bible days, pitchers were generally used to carry water. A woman placed the pitcher on her head to take it to her family. When the old pitcher cracked, the water ran all over the place. This, too, is a description of old age. When we are young, our pitcher is in great shape. We need to carry water in it then when we can do some good—not wait until it's broken and cracked with age.

One final figure emerges in verse 6: "the wheel [is] broken at the well." Have you ever seen a wheel lifting water out of a well? A new wheel does the job beautifully. But as the wheel ages it begins to fall apart, creaking and groaning until it finally collapses and it can no longer lift water. That's another picture of old age and added reason for doing what we can while we are young.

Teens Can Be God's Most Genuine People

Some years ago a lady told me a story about her husband and son. She said, "My husband took our eleven-year-old son in a canoe up the Amazon River, where they visited a lot of tribal groups. Wherever they went, people came out of their huts to ask my husband to pray for their sick loved ones. Our son stood by as his daddy laid his hands on people and prayed for them."

In the end, the boy asked his father, "Daddy, why don't they go to a doctor?"

His father replied, "Because there isn't a doctor within a thousand miles of here."

The boy said earnestly, "Daddy, when I grow up, I am going to be that doctor."

Not long ago that "boy" met me at an airport in Colombia, South America. He is now a plastic surgeon there, specializing in reconstructive surgery. The boy saw a need and despite being so young, he had a sense of calling. Young people need to be encouraged to recognize their teenage years as a time for vision and involvement—preparation and an excited looking forward to life, instead of goofing off and generally postponing the business of being a human being.

I sincerely believe that teenagers are looking for genuine life. They are truthful and want to do the right thing. They also want their lives to count. And when teenagers become convinced about something, they can be the most conscientious, sincere workers and thinkers on the planet. But they need assistance and encouragement, because growing up can be a frightening prospect. Moving into the unknown areas and stages of life can be intimidating. Teenagers can display a lot of bravado and nonchalance, but they are often haunted by insecurity. We can help them recognize that, although they are in the process of growing up and under a lot of pressure, they have tremendous potential. They need to know that we have confidence in them.

We can also help our teens assume the responsibility of self-control. Self-control grows as wisdom grows. Not only do teens have potential, but they have the strength and the ability to make decisions and stick by them. They are able to maintain healthy attitudes and avoid illegitimate activities. If true confidence and purpose are built into their lives, they can work independently enough to reject hero worship and resist the wrong kind of peer pressure. But all of these qualities grow best with the encouragement, example, and instruction from adults in a teen's life.

Ultimately, teens need to concern themselves with personal development. This is accomplished by developing healthy peer relationships, which build people up rather than pull them down. Personal development includes maintaining physical well-being and nurturing spiritual growth. In a world where so many people go aimlessly through life, without any guiding principles or standards beyond satisfying their immediate desires, our teenagers will be making strides ahead of the rest simply by learning to live by a solid set of values. The best boost we can give them is a strong purpose in life—the purpose we find in living out our destiny as God's genuine people. Real teenagers don't fake it or flaunt the values of their parents. Instead, they think for themselves. In the crucible of life, they make the tough decisions and become mature people of God.

Let's Get Practical

1. What have you found to be the most tumultuous aspects of the teen years?

2. How are teenagers "people in process" in the following areas, and what support can we offer as they grow and develop?

    psychologically:

    physically:

    spiritually:

    socially:

3. In what situations do teenagers face pressure, and how can parents, friends, and other people be supportive at these times?

4. List some ways parents, teachers, and friends can help young people discover and develop their potential.

5. When you were a teenager, what helped you the most in your growth as a person and as a Christian? As you look back, what do you think *would have been* helpful to you?

6. How will you use your own experiences and memories of adolescence to help you be a true encourager to the teens you know?

6

People Who Don't Marry Are Just As Real

In the church of Jesus Christ there is a tremendous emphasis on marriage and the family, and rightly so. But because of this emphasis, not infrequently single people in the church gain the impression—whether it is given intentionally or not—that they are less than whole people.

By "singles," I mean those who are not married, either by choice or by chance. Some people are unmarried because they choose not to be, and some are not married because of various things that have happened to them that were not of their choosing.

How has America changed insofar as the marital status of its people is concerned? Single households in the United States increased 66 percent between 1960 and 1980. In the adult population in the United States, presently 43 million people are single. Of those, 22 million have never married, 10 million are widowed, and 11 million are divorced and have not remarried. So we are talking about a large segment of American society that is, for one reason or another, single at the present time. Twenty percent of the people attending the church of which I am pastor are single. Obviously, when we look at these figures, we recognize that the issue of singleness needs to be addressed from a biblical perspective.

Singleness and Scripture

The Bible tells us about some very famous single people. Jesus was single. It is something of a surprise to those who are married to realize that if Jesus Christ attended their church he would probably go to one of the singles' studies. Not only that. The apostle Paul would probably be in the same group, because he was single too. Why the apostle was single, we are not sure. But that he was appears evident. Some students of the Bible say he was a member of the Sanhedrin, and to be in the Sanhedrin, he had to be married. Therefore, if he was now single, when he was serving the Savior, either his wife had died or, possibly, when converted to Christ, his wife left him. In one of his autobiographical passages, Paul says for the sake of Christ he suffered the loss of "all things," and that everything that was dear to him he counted but as refuse for the excellency of the knowledge of Christ. However, it is only a theory that Paul was married before his conversion.

Adam was single for a period of time—but he didn't do very well with it. The Scriptures begin by saying that God evaluated everything he had made and said that it was good. But then he stepped back from his creation, looked at Adam living a single life, and said that it was not good.

Outstanding among the women of the Bible who were single is the delightful lady named Anna. You find her in the beginning of Luke's Gospel. She was married seven years and then was widowed, and she lived until she was eighty-four. So she was a widow a long, long time, but she devoted her widowhood to a powerful ministry.

The Scriptures talk favorably of single people. But the texts need to be read and understood within their contexts. Genesis 2:18, for example, says, "It is not good for the man to be alone." But Matthew 19 says that "it is better not to marry." And 1 Corinthians 7:26 also says that it is good to remain single.

I point out those three passages to remind us that when we look into the Bible, it is imperative that we *think*. Some people say that all we have to do is believe the Bible, but if we are just going to "believe" the Bible, without thinking about what it says, we could be believing all kinds of things. I could quote the Bible and say categorically, "The Bible says it is good not to marry." It does say that, but to take that out of its context without presenting the other balancing aspects of the truth would be to distort what the Bible says.

First of all, the Genesis passage refers to God's evaluation of Adam in his single state. God has ordained from Creation that people would be male and female. He ordained this so that they might have companionship, because creatures were created for relationship. Therefore, it is normative in the creation order for there to be a relationship between male and female, and God has said that this relationship should flourish into marriage.

One reason, of course, for marriage is that in this heterosexual relationship children would be born, and the human race would propagate itself. So in Genesis 2:18 we come up with a general rule: It is right that people should be married and that they should have families. If we stop there, we make every single person feel less than normal. But, of course, Scripture has other things to teach us on the subject.

In Matthew, the disciples say, "It is better not to marry" (19:10). The background to this is that the Pharisees were trying to trap the Lord Jesus into a debate on divorce. But the Lord would not fall into their trap, insisting rather that he is not in favor of a flippant approach to divorce or a casual acceptance of remarriage. He answered: "I tell you that anyone who divorces his wife, except for marital unfaithfulness, and marries another woman commits adultery" (v. 9, NIV). Now that's straightforward enough, but it is not all of the biblical teaching on divorce and remarriage.

Notice the reaction of the disciples. They say, "If this is the situation between a husband and wife, it is better not to marry." Now there is the quote. In other words, the disciples responded with incredulity to the statement that Jesus had just made. And the Lord then responded to their incredulous amazement by adding, "Not everyone can accept this word. . . . Some are eunuchs because they were born that way; others were made that way by men; and others have renounced marriage because of the kingdom of heaven. The one who can accept this should accept it" (vv. 11-12, NIV).

Jesus is saying that it is perfectly legitimate to be single, but that there are different reasons for singleness. Some people, he said, are born with the propensity toward singleness, some have been put into that situation by other people, and others have chosen singleness.

This reminds me of the quote from Shakespeare's Twelfth Night: "Some are born great, some achieve greatness, and some have greatness thrust upon them." I suppose that you could say that some people are born single, some people achieve singleness, and others have singleness thrust upon them.

The Lord Jesus is outlining something very special in Matthew 19:11-12. He is saying that those who choose singleness for the sake of the kingdom are very special people indeed. This idea is amplified in 1 Corinthians 7:7, where Paul says, "I wish that all men were as I am. But each man has his own gift from God; one has this gift, another has that" (NIV). Paul is saying that singleness can be a high calling, given by God to some people as a special gift.

This is not my theory; it is a biblical statement. The Bible teaches that singleness for some people is a high calling and that some people are gifted of God to function in that particular state. Let me give a few examples of this. I think all of us recognize that some kinds of missionary work can be done adequately only by single people. Some of the most remarkable people you will read about anywhere are women missionaries who embraced singleness with a sense of high calling, accepted it as a gift from God, and utilized it for his glory.

Every Christmas there is a special offering in Southern Baptist churches called the Lottie Moon offering, devoted entirely to foreign missions. It was initiated by Lottie Moon when she tried to mobilize women to have an interest in missions. She had had the opportunity to marry a certain gentleman, Crawford Toy, a notable Old Testament theologian. He wanted to marry Lottie, but according to Lottie he had been infected by the thinking of German theologians and was theologically unsound. She could not see how he could possibly assist her in the ministry she had given herself to in China. Therefore, she embraced singleness, literally for the sake of the kingdom. Toy went on to become a distinguished professor of Old Testament at Harvard Divinity School, and Lottie, as she put it, trudged her lonely way in China.

The impact of Lottie Moon's life lives on. Now, during every Christmas season, the Lottie Moon Christmas offering for missions averages 20 million dollars. Good old Lottie—a single woman, who for the sake of the kingdom embraced her singleness and gave herself to ministering.

Amy Carmichael went out from England to India, and lived fifty-five years in India without a furlough. She spent the last twenty years of her missionary service mainly on her back as an invalid after a serious injury she sustained in a fall. Amy Carmichael struggled with her singleness, but she eventually accepted that this was what God had in mind for her so that she might devote herself to a lifestyle that others were not prepared to share.

There was a system in India at that time (in the late nineteenth century) in which young girls were taken into the temples and trained to become temple prostitutes. Amy went into the temples, brought those girls out, and provided orphanages for them. She started the Dohnavur Fellowship, which goes on to this day. Amy Carmichael embraced singleness as a high calling, believing that God had given her the gift. It was not her choice, but she accepted it and utilized it for the good of the kingdom.

Another single woman missionary who illustrates this truth was Gladys Aylward. She stood about 4 feet 11, on tiptoe. Working at a very menial job in England, she applied to the China Island Mission to go to China as a missionary. But they turned her down because she had a learning disability. When the mission told her that she could not go to China, she said that God had told her to go. So she packed two suitcases, donned a coat, bought a railway ticket from London to China, and traveled across Europe, Russia, and Siberia into China with her two suitcases. In her luggage she packed two saucepans and a cooking stove, and she clanked along carrying her two suitcases, one of which was full of food for the journey. As she reached Siberia, she discovered that a war was raging between the Russians and the Chinese and the only people traveling on the rails were soldiers. They kicked her off, but she climbed back on again. She found herself literally in the middle of the fighting, and the train wasn't going any further. So she got off the train with her two suitcases and her pack of pots and pans and walked along the tracks toward China.

I heard Gladys Aylward tell her story one night in England—her life has been described in a biography called *The Small Woman* and depicted on film in a semiaccurate movie called *The Inn of the Sixth Happiness*. She said that God had promised her all that she needed, so she said, "God, I need a husband. Send him out here." For years she prayed for God to meet this need, she said. Then she peered over the pulpit—and she could barely see over it—and pointed and shouted at the young people listening to this fiery little lady and said, "Somewhere in this world, there is a man to whom God said, 'Go to China and marry Gladys.' And he never came." I could see a number of young men slipping down in their seats. Gladys Aylward had a remarkable ministry in China for many, many years—as a single person.

These illustrations show, as the Scriptures teach, that it is good for some not to marry for the sake of the kingdom, and that is a high calling.

Scripture goes on to say that singleness produces its own un-usual pressures. Loneliness is certainly one. Another is sexuality—how to handle one's God-given sexual drives. A third factor is bitterness or resentment over having to live a single life. Most single people experience a sense of worthlessness or rejection. This may be felt by singles because no one ever wanted to marry them or because they were married and were deserted and divorced. Sometimes singles have to combat a sense of selfishness when they have chosen to be single for reasons that are less than noble. These are some of the problems that single people have to confront. Even those who say they have embraced singleness as a gift from God, as a high calling for the sake of the kingdom, will tell you that they are not immune to these pains and pressures.

John Stott, from whose ministry so many of us have benefitted, is single. On his sixtieth birthday, someone asked him at what age he decided that God had given him the gift of singleness. He said, "Fifty-nine." He was saying that for the sake of the kingdom, he would embrace singleness. But he was also hinting at the fact that singleness is not easy. And nobody ever suggested that it would be.

However, having said that, 1 Corinthians 7 also tells us that singleness offers a special freedom. The apostle Paul could pack his bag and take off on a missionary journey, and nobody would know where he was, how long he was to be gone, or what he was up to. When he showed up again, it was fine; he didn't have family responsibilities. There are some people who for the sake of the kingdom will say, "God has given me special freedom, and I will utilize it for what is noble and eternal.

Singleness also bestows new and unusual opportunities on the single person. If the single person has fewer responsibilities, he or she may have more resources, more time, and more energy to do something positive. That, clearly, is what Paul is teaching in 1 Corinthians 7.

Singleness and Society

When you look at secular society and the attitude toward single people so often conveyed by the media, it is obvious that those who orchestrate the ad campaigns have learned that a lot of singles are out there who have money and are bent on spending it. If you look at much of the advertising that is being directed toward singles, you discover that the image being projected is one of freedom and fulfillment. There is nothing quite so exciting, these advertisements would say, as being free and fulfilled. The approach is basically: no commitments, no ties, no restraints. "Get out there and live it up! Why bother yourself with all kinds of responsibilities?" Lots of people would like to be free and to feel fulfilled; they would like to have no commitments and be rid of all restraints, particularly if they think that route leads to the fulfilled life.

Many single people in our society have followed this theory. However, this particular philosophy is a fraud. The idea is that you can have companionship without commitment. Obviously, everybody wants companionship, and many are looking for this companionship without commitment. The movie *Looking for Mr. Goodbar* is a very dramatic demonstration of this. It is the story of a young woman who was a very fine school teacher by day, but who went the rounds of the single bars at night, looking for companionship without commitment. She found companionship, but she ended up being used. Voices in our secular society say that you can have meaningful experiences, but you don't necessarily have to have ties. They tell you that you can be fulfilled without doing anything that has lasting significance. And that simply is not true.

Singles in the secular society are beginning to question the philosophy of what was touted as "the single lifestyle." Many of them have been so busy having a good time that they are exhausted; others are bored. A number have gotten into things that have produced guilt in their lives. They question whether they can continue doing what they like, because they are afraid of the consequences, namely the risk of being exposed to an STD or AIDS. So, we have a large population of single people who are beginning to wonder if what they thought was fun isn't a big fraud. Who would be more reachable with the gracious message of forgiveness and joy and peace in Christ than these "exhausted, bored, guilty, frightened" people? Incidentally, those are not my words; they are the very words that single people outside the church are using to describe themselves.

Singleness and the Church

Many single people have told me that they feel the church is not always sympathetic to the single person. Quite understandably, the church has a strong and persistent emphasis on marriage and the family. We have to endorse that. But at the same time we should listen, putting ourselves in the place of persons who are not married and who do not have children. If they see all of our church programs being family oriented, and if they hear only messages expounding what the Bible teaches about marriage, how are they to react? Not infrequently they will think that this fellowship is not particularly sympathetic to the unique needs and concerns of the single person.

Sometimes church people demonstrate suspicion of the single person. This can be seen, for instance, in a small group of believers, all of whom are happily married, when an attractive young divorcee is introduced to the group. Some people in the group will try to get to know this young woman, but you will find that if the men try to help, the wives of those men will become suspicious. They may hate themselves for it, but they will be concerned and feel threatened. And the divorcee will sense what is going on and feel very unwelcome.

What happens when a single person begins to attend and it is learned that he or she (who may be thirty or forty) has never been married? Some Christians are afflicted with homophobia, and they might suspect that the newcomer is homosexual. Nothing is said, but the thought is there, and the distance is there. It seems to me that few churches know how to include the "eligible" person in their activities and how to welcome them nonjudgmentally.

The third thing that often happens to the unmarried person coming into the church community is that he or she senses there is insensitivity toward the single person's feelings. A number of years ago, a young single lady came on our staff as church secretary. As it happened, on the particular Sunday she was welcomed by our fellowship, I was teaching out of 1 Corinthians 7. So I was preaching on singleness, and I dealt with many of the things that I am talking about in this chapter.

At the end of the service, one little lady went up to our new secretary and said, "Welcome, Glenda. We are so happy to have you here. Are you married?"

Glenda said, "No, I'm not."

"Well," the woman responded, "Don't worry about it. We'll soon find you a nice husband!" To which Glenda responded, "Madam, I suggest you listen to the exposition of the Word of God."

What I had been trying to explain that day was that some people are called to singleness and that they are not to be regarded insensitively; nor are they to be regarded with pity. It is just possible, I had tried to point out, that they are very special people whom God wants in that particular state; and it is insulting to suggest that they must have a mate.

Insensitivity, suspicion, and a lack of sympathy—these are attitudes that often confront the single person in the Christian community. Now if that is true, and if all I have said about the single in secular society is true, then ministering to singles inside and outside the church should be one of the top concerns of a healthy church.

Singleness and the Single

Single persons need to evaluate their status or calling. A single man or woman needs to look into his or her heart and ask, *Do I deeply resent my singleness? Am I rejecting my singleness? Is my major concern to change my singleness? Or have I come to the point of accepting that for now, in God's economy, he wants me single? That being the case, I will embrace my singleness as a high calling with unique opportunities and unique privileges, and I will take it from him, believing that he will gift me for it.* It seems to me that in the light of Scripture, the single person needs to come to that point.

Unmarried people need to be realistic in identifying the cause of their singleness. Are you unmarried by choice or by chance? It may be that you have been widowed, and it was something thrust upon you. You may have been divorced. Maybe you didn't want it to happen, and you tried to avoid it, but it happened, and here you are. Perhaps you have been deserted. Your mate just walked out on you, and now you suddenly discover after many years that you are single and don't know what to do with your singleness. I can't think of anything much sadder than the person who has been married for twenty years and who is suddenly dropped like a hot potato. Several have come and talked to me about how to handle dating when you are in your forties. Then, of course, there are people who are single because, for a variety of reasons, they never had the opportunity to meet somebody who wanted to share life with them.

If you are single, you must look at the situation and come to terms with it. In light of what Scripture teaches about singleness, if I am widowed, can I accept now this singleness imposed upon me? If I am divorced, or whatever might be my case, will I accept the situation at this time? And in so doing, will I believe that God will gift and equip me for it?

What about those who are single by choice? Why do some people choose to be single? Some do because of shyness—they just don't know how to relate to other people, and so they choose to keep out of harm's way. Others are afraid of what might happen. They have observed their parents' bad marriage. They have seen the terrible things that people can do to each other and have decided, *No way. Wild horses wouldn't drag me into a situation like that.* Such shyness and fear need to be dealt with.

What about people who have immature attitudes and because of that have never married? They just haven't grown up, and because they haven't, it is demonstrated in many ways. Some say homosexuality is not so much an aberration as an arrested or retarded development. As children grow up, there are times in the adolescent years when a boy is more interested in a boy, and a girl is more interested in a girl. If parents try to get the boys interested in girls, or the girls interested in boys at this stage, it is no use. They hate each other. But what if something traumatic happens in the young person's life at that time? If there is an arresting of the emotional development, is it possible that things for that person don't develop from that moment on, and he or she never makes a normal adaptation toward the opposite sex? It's only a theory, and it will not absolve a person from the responsibility of sin—and homosexual behavior is sin—but it could be that some people choose not to be married for such a reason. Maybe it is fear, or arrested development, or shyness. I believe that single people need to come to terms with their singleness, evaluate it, and then live in the light of Scripture's teaching.

How do we handle the bitterness? By identifying whom we are bitter against concerning our state of singleness. If we believe that somebody else is responsible for it, are we coming to the point of forgiveness?

How do we handle the pressures of sexuality? In obedience to standards given us in the Word of God. When the Bible talks about singleness, it is assuming celibacy. It is not talking about the singleness that is in vogue now, where single people want the benefits of marriage without the responsibilities. When the Bible talks about being single, it is talking about being celibate. Sexual purity is assumed.

How do we handle any sense of unworthiness or rejection, or the feeling that we are not very attractive? I've got one simple suggestion. If a single person, or anyone, is struggling with low-self esteem, I encourage such people to become active in children's ministries. If you give yourself to those kids, you will begin to discover that you are of inestimable worth to them. You may never have children of your own, but that is not to say that you cannot invest yourself in the lives of a lot of other kids. In our church, a high percentage of the kids in our Sunday school are from single-parent families. They have tremendous needs. And it may well be that some of the single people in any of our churches who are wallowing in a sense of worthlessness could discover a new purpose for living by giving themselves to kids.

What about selfishness? The only way I know to handle selfishness is to look at what I have and realize that it came from the Lord for his purposes, so that I won't squander it. As I look at my freedom, my resources, and my energy, whether I am single or married, I must accept that they are given me for God's glory, and I am eternally accountable for how I use them.

I trust that those who are single might be able to look into their singleness, look carefully at its unique consequences, and find out how, in the power of the Spirit, to use their singleness—and the opportunities it presents—for the glory of God.

Let's Get Practical

1. How are single people alienated and discouraged by society? by family? by church people?

2. What is God's view of people who don't marry, according to Scripture?

3. Where does God's view of singleness conflict with prevailing opinion out in "the world"?

4. List some means by which the church can become a friendlier place for unmarried people.

5. What resources does God offer to the single person? What opportunities are sometimes made possible by a state of singleness?

7

Genuine Friends:
Necessities or Luxuries?

In *The Seasons of a Man's Life*, Daniel Levinson says, "Friendship is largely noticeable by its absence. Close friendship with a man or woman is rarely experienced by American men." Levinson is, of course, dealing particularly with men, but the problem is broader in scope. Those who are concerned about our society recognize that we are often impoverished because of the superficiality of our relationships.

Scripture makes it very clear that our lives are lived in terms of relationships—with God and with human beings. These relationships operate at many different levels, but in this chapter we will try to answer the question "Are real friends necessities or luxuries?" Friendship is a crucial aspect of our lives, and the Bible has much to say about it.

The Divine Dimension

Although I'm afraid most of us don't often reflect on it, the Christian's best friend of all is God himself. We lowly humans can have a relationship with the living God. I can't imagine a more exciting opportunity.

The Bible frequently talks about people who were "friends" of God. The book of Exodus tells us that God used to "speak to Moses face to face, as a man speaks with his friend" (33:11, NIV). This figurative expression means heart-to-heart communication, with the closeness of dear friends, not just passing acquaintances.

God spoke to Abraham in a unique way; in Scripture he is called "the friend of God." But the statement that we can perhaps relate to more than these is what our Lord Jesus says in John 15, when he talks to his disciples. He reminds them that he is their master, their Lord, their Savior, and that they are his servants. But then he says, "I'm not going to talk to you as if you're my servants; I'm going to talk to you as if you're my friends." And in a very beautiful and special way, he shows them that he has opened his heart to them.

The Scriptures point out to us, however, that if we are to be the friends of God, and if we are to regard the Lord Jesus as a particular and special friend, we need to bear something in mind. I am thinking of what James says: "Don't you know that friendship with the world is hatred toward God?" Anyone who chooses to be a friend of the world becomes an enemy of God. God says he would love to have a friendship with us; the Lord Jesus says that he calls his servants his friends because of the intimacy of relationship they have developed. But we are reminded that we cannot regard God and his Christ as our friends if we are committed to that whole system that is so unfriendly toward him—what the Scriptures call "the world." A secular attitude toward life is to a very large extent opposed to friendship with the Lord Jesus.

It will be worthwhile to look into our own hearts at this point and ask: *Do I relate to God as my friend? Do I feel that there's heart-to-heart communication with him? Is there a two-way honesty and transparency between us?*

We can go even further: *Do I relate to the Lord Jesus as my friend? Do I regard him in a very special way, as one who did what nobody would dare to do—lay down his life for his friends? And can I respond and honestly say that I regard him as my intimate friend?* We ought to be able to identify our spiritual relationship at this level.

The Human Dimension

Now let's move to the relationship of one human being to another. Richard Fowler, in an article in *Discipleship Journal*, points out that friendships operate at five different levels.

First of all, he talks about the *generality* stage. This is the stage of first encounter, when we bump up against somebody whom we have never seen.

Now, having bumped into this person for the first time, it may be that we say to ourselves, *Hmmmm, I'd like to get to know him (or her) better.* It is equally possible that our reaction is, *Yuck! Let's get out of here as quickly as we can.*

Fowler says that, according to scientific observation, 30 percent of the people we meet in these first encounters dislike us immediately. We don't have to say a word; they are just turned right off.

Recognizing this, we should find encouragement in knowing that 70 percent evidently think we're not so bad. And for both these groups, we can tell ourselves to relax. There's the possibility of getting to know them at a different level.

Second, Fowler talks about the *accommodating* level. This level is not as superficial as bumping elbows, but it is still only what might be called an arm's-length relationship. For whatever reasons, we find ourselves with these people. And while we want to get along with them—something about them is attractive and interesting—we have no initial intention of developing any degree of intimate relationship with them.

This can be seen often in a church congregation. And the problem with this arm's-length relationship is that there's a minimum of reality in it. There's a lot of superficiality, a lot of play-acting, a lot of projecting. On the accommodating level we deal basically with perceptions; we don't really know the person and he or she doesn't know us, but we sort of get along. If we are operating at that level, there is the possibility that we can press through to the third level of friendship: the *teamwork* stage.

You and someone with whom you may have been "bumping elbows" find a common objective. And you begin to discover that now you are not just at arm's length; you are putting your shoulders to a common task. As a result you begin to experience a certain camaraderie. And when you do, you find that the relationship becomes more realistic.

Some years ago our church people recognized how large our congregation was becoming, so we divided our people into small groups. We encouraged people to get into small groups in order to be nurtured, so that they might care for one another. People began putting their shoulders under a common load and as a result came to know each other as they never had before. For two years most of the groups met regularly, with good results. But something happened that most of these people didn't expect. As they got past the stage of superficial pretense, some acknowledged that they disliked others in the group. "We would rather have nothing to do with one another," they would tell me.

At that point they began to level with each other and minister to each other—and the possibility existed of moving into the fourth stage of friendship. Fowler calls this the *significant other* stage.

Out of their group, some began to discover a certain compatibility, a certain commonality. And they began to open up more and more to each other, to such an extent that they got past the like-and-dislike stage. They got to where they could trust their newfound friend. They could even be vulnerable with the other person, knowing that he or she would probably be vulnerable in return. In this way, they began to discover something mutually beneficial in the relationship.

Now it is highly improbable that a person has this kind of relationship with more than ten or fifteen people in a lifetime. But when you do, you can press beyond that stage into the fifth level— the *intimate* or very-best-friend stage. At this level, which you might expect to experience with one or two people, you have such intimacy that just about anything goes in terms of concern and support and nurture for one another.

The Bible, as I have said, has a lot to say on the subject of friendship, and it suggests quite forcibly that we ought to be cooperating on all of these five levels if we are to be properly encouraged, nurtured, and supported. Let's look more closely at the relationships in which we can expect to experience friendships at these levels.

Male-female relationships

First, there is the intimate friendship of a man and a woman. If you're a married person, it is hoped that your spouse is your very best friend. You two are long past the bumping-elbows, arm's-length, and common-objective stages. You have seen things about each other that are mutually attractive and mutually beneficial, and you have come to the point of commitment and transparency. As intimate friends you are constantly nurturing and encouraging each other.

This is suggested to us powerfully in Proverbs 2:17 (NIV). Speaking about an adulteress, the writer says she is "a wayward wife with her seductive words who has left the partner of her youth and ignored the covenant she made before God." The word translated "partner" is translated in other passages as "close friend," suggesting that the person to whom you are married should be your partner, your close friend, the one with whom you have intimacy. One of the most enriching things that can happen to a man or woman is to have a marital relationship that is based, among other things, on a very intimate friendship, in which you thoroughly enjoy each other.

There are three things that usually lead to friendship. If I see something good, something pleasant, something useful in the other person, then it is likely that I will be drawn in friendship toward that person. If two people are married they ought to be seeing in each other what is good, pleasant, and useful; on this basis a man and a woman can have a very intimate relationship. In marriage they should. However, is this the only area in which a man and a woman can have a healthy relationship?

Daniel Levinson says, "Most men have not had an intimate,

nonsexual friendship with a woman." I was talking to a group of young single women from our church, and they told me that one of their problems is that they would like very much to make friends with young men on a nonromantic, nonsexual basis. They told me they would like to learn how to relate to Christian men and to know the mutual encouragement of such a relationship, but it is awkward and difficult.

It is possibly even more awkward and difficult for married people to develop helpful relationships with members of the opposite sex, because they can easily go wrong. In addition, because so many people assume the worst about people and promptly put a wrong interpretation on things, it is rare to find married people having close friendships with other people of the opposite sex.

However, I think that if we cannot have relationships with people of the opposite sex on a nonromantic, nonsexual basis, we are impoverished as a result. The church of Jesus Christ gives us a magnificent opportunity for developing these healthy, helpful relationships. The Lord Jesus himself illustrated this. On numerous occasions in the Gospels we read of the close friendships he had with women. And this was something that was even more out of the ordinary in his day.

Friendships between women and between men

Anyone who has observed the female scene will recognize that women appear to have an easier time of making friends than do men. They seem to be more open to developing relationships. Sometime ago, my wife, Jill, wrote a book called *Thank You for Being a Friend*. While she was writing that book I was helping refresh her memory about certain relationships she had had over the years, and it was intriguing to me how many different, rich relationships that Jill has enjoyed. I remember thinking that men do not experience friendship in the same way very often.

What about friendships between men? Levinson, in the book I referred to earlier, writes, "Most men do not have an intimate male friend of the kind they recall fondly from boyhood." It's a sad commentary on our society that now a man who has a close relationship with another man is suspected of being homosexual. That is more a commentary on our perverted society than it is on the validity of close man-to-man relationships. Perhaps we men aren't open to this kind of thing because we recognize that it requires time and sacrifice, transparency and honesty. And very often we are not prepared to accept the vulnerability that is identified with those qualities. As a result, men often know nothing of a relationship such as that between David and Jonathan (1 Sam. 18–20). There are many instances of healthy, man-to-man friendships in Scripture; for example, Peter and John, Paul and Barnabas, and Abraham and Lot.

The friendship of youth and mature age

One of the lovely illustrations in the New Testament of friendship between an older person and a younger one is the relationship that existed between Barnabas and John Mark. Barnabas was the older colleague of the apostle Paul, and John Mark was the young fellow who left them on their first missionary journey. He blew it. When Paul said that he wanted nothing more to do with John Mark, Barnabas stuck with him. He chose John Mark to go with him, the friendship was nurtured, and they continued working together.

I look back, with tremendous gratitude, to a man who came into my life when I was a young teenager, during the Second World War. He was at least thirty years older than me. I was beginning to question Christianity, particularly the brand I had been introduced to as a boy. I didn't question the faith of my father and mother; I knew their faith was genuine, and I embraced it and endorsed it heartily. It was just that their particular expression of it seemed dull to me.

But one morning this man marched into our little church, resplendent in the uniform of the Royal Artillery. He was a captain, all man, and he became my friend. He went out of his way to befriend me, and he still writes me regularly. He's in his middle eighties now, and he still tells me exactly what I need to hear, whether I want to hear it or not. He has not changed at all in his total commitment to me and interest in me. For forty years I have known this relationship, and I am extremely grateful for it. Do you have these different kinds of friendships? They are so enriching, so necessary.

The friendship of youth and youth

One of the interesting features about Augustine's *Confessions* is that he was mortified by some of the things he did as a youth. He had a remarkably sensitive conscience, and some things pressed heavily upon him. For instance, he was upset before God that he had stolen some fruit as a boy. He devotes quite a lot of space in his *Confessions* to that. Interestingly, he identifies peer pressure as a big factor in this incident. The bad friendships he had made led him into that kind of behavior.

We know that young people can have very negative peer pressure. If young people identify with other youths who have an unhealthy influence over them, there is a high possibility they will go wrong, because in adolescence what their friends think is more important to them that what their parents say.

But peer pressure is not all wrong. Being one of the most powerful influences, it can actually help. That's why it is so important that young people develop the right friendships and that parents commit themselves to seeing that they do.

Parents who want their kids to grow up to be healthy, mature Christians make the effort to ensure that they are surrounded by healthy, growing young Christians. We shouldn't expect our youth to develop a mature Christian lifestyle if they spend most of their time with unbelieving kids—if we let them run wild because we can't be bothered, or because we are more interested in their playing ball than getting into a youth group. If we want them to grow up well, we must make sure they have positive peer pressure, because the friendships of youth with other youth can be profoundly helpful.

The Prize of Friendship

What's in it for me? That is the question, of course, that immediately comes to mind when we consider the sacrifices that go with friendship. If I'm going to have to give of myself, be vulnerable, be open—if I'm going to be prepared to nurture people, work with them, and spend time with them—what is in it for me?

First of all, friendships give us the opportunity of fulfilling our longing for belonging. This desire is in every human being. No one, deep down, wants to be regarded as irrelevant or insignificant. No one wants to think, *If anything happened to me today, nobody would miss me.* We would feel devastated if we believed that we could disappear off the face of this earth without anyone even noticing.

The Scripture says that in friendships this longing for belonging can be very wonderfully met. Proverbs 17:17 says, "A friend loves at all times, and a brother is born for adversity" (NIV). Having somebody who will always love you and be with you through difficult times—this is part of the prize that is friendship.

Proverbs 18:24 says, "A man of many companions may come to ruin, but there is a friend who sticks closer than a brother" (NIV). To have friends like that is to be rich indeed.

In Ecclesiastes 4:9-12 (NIV), we read these words, some of which are applicable to friendship, and some of which apply specifically to marriage:

Two are better than one, because they have a good return for their work: If one falls down, his friend can help him up. But pity the man who falls and has no one to help him up! Also, if two lie down together they will keep warm. But how can one keep warm alone? Though one may be overpowered, two can defend themselves. A cord of three strands is not quickly broken.

This passage says, in effect, that there are definite benefits for the person who takes the time to build friendships with others. A primary benefit is the growth and maturity that happen in us when we are committed to such a relationship:

> Wounds from a friend can be trusted, but an enemy multiplies kisses. . . . Perfume and incense bring joy to the heart, and the pleasantness of one's friend springs from his earnest counsel. (Prov. 27:6, 9, NIV)

Two delightful expressions here remind us that when genuine friendships are developed: a friend's counsel is helpful and brings joy; but a real friend sometimes will tell us what we do not want to hear. In such circumstances, "faithful are the wounds of a friend."

How do we grow? By developing relationships in which we demonstrate loving concern for each other. As we develop this loving concern, we counsel each other. If a relationship has been established, we hear what we need to hear, not just what we want to hear. And because of the relationship, we accept what our friend says and respond accordingly.

One day, Mr. Langton, a good friend of the brilliant Dr. Samuel Johnson, wanted to point out something to Dr. Johnson: "You have a habit of contradicting people in conversation," he said.

Johnson responded, "And what's wrong with that?"

Langton said, "Nothing particularly, except the way in which you do it is hard for sensitive souls to bear."

"If they're sensitive," Johnson responded, "they need to bear something in order to grow up."

The discussion developed into an argument, and Langton decided not to pursue it further. Rather, he chose to write a number of texts on a piece of paper for Johnson.

The texts he wrote out were these: "Blessed are the meek." "With all lowliness and meekness . . . endeavoring to keep the unity of the Spirit." "Love suffereth long . . . is kind . . . is not puffed up."

Taking the slip of paper from his friend who had dared challenge him, Johnson went home. Upon reaching there, he read the texts and realized that his friend was right. So he returned to Langton and apologized, saying that changes needed to be made. That's friendship—when someone will honestly level with you, giving you the opportunity to know what is wrong and how you can put it right.

Friendship takes risks. But counterfeit friendship won't risk at all; people in such relationships simply pretend that everything is fine.

Someone has said, cynically, that there is no man so friendless but what he can find a friend sincere enough to tell him disagreeable truth. That is true. Unfortunately, some people feel it their God-given responsibility to communicate disagreeable truth to people whom they don't know and therefore cannot possibly care about.

My former colleague Joe Ballard once said to me, "Always earn the right to rebuke somebody before you do it." And then he said, "Before you earn the right to rebuke people, you have got to show them that you are primarily concerned with their well-being." Do you have friends like that? If you don't, you are probably remaining at the same level. You go on making the same mistakes, doing the same injurious things, and you never discover that a major benefit of friendship is growth. The ultimate benefit of friendship is the fulfillment of your "longing for belonging." It is the assurance that someone will be with you in adversity, and it almost guarantees you growth and maturity.

The prize of friendship also includes the privileges of sharing:

The poor are shunned even by their neighbors,
but the rich have many friends.
He who despises his neighbor sins,
but blessed is he who is kind to the needy. (Prov. 14:20-21, NIV)

Rich people do have many friends, although the word *friends* sometimes comes into question. Very often the celebrities who have people hanging around them—wealthy people who have lots of people buzzing around them—are the most lonely people in the world. Why? Because all the time they are wondering if their "friends" are real friends. And very often such people have the feeling that it's not them that people want, but their money; it is not them, but the reflected glory of the celebrity they seek.

Proverbs is absolutely right. The rich have many friends, but those who are kind to the needy are the real friends. A friend in need is a friend indeed. We demonstrate the genuineness of our friendship, not by identifying with those whom we feel are going to greatly benefit us, but by identifying with those who need our encouragement and support.

The Price of Friendship

Everything worth something costs something, and friendship has its particular costs. First of all, as far as making friends is concerned, we must accept the fact that not everyone can be our best friend. You don't have the time and energy to have lots of best friends. And those whom you've decided are going to be your best friends may have no intention of being that. As we've said, friendships operate at different levels.

Let me illustrate this from the life of the Lord Jesus. When he fed five thousand men and their families, I'm sure that those people were all disposed in a friendly way toward him. If you had asked him then, "Do you have any friends?" he could have said, "Oh, look at my friends—thousands of them, all over the place."

He obviously couldn't develop very close relationships with all of those people, and so out of that great crowd he chose seventy. He spent some time with the seventy, and having taught them and trained them, he sent them out two by two. But seventy is a large number of people to get close to. So he picked out twelve and really spent a lot of time with those twelve.

But it is interesting that when he was in distress and under pressure, he drew to himself three of the twelve. These were his close, intimate friends. This illustrates to us that friendships operate at different levels even among the twelve disciples.

If we're going to make friends, we have to understand that friendships grow, mature, and develop. They start with the five thousand. They narrow down to the seventy, and then to the twelve, and eventually to three, but only time and work will determine that.

When we are making friends, we ought to be realistic about what kind of friendship we are talking about. There are some dangers to watch for. Proverbs is full of healthy warnings in this regard. We need to be careful of what kind of friends we make.

> My son, if you have put up security for your neighbor,
> [or your friend]
> if you have struck hands in pledge for another,
> if you have been trapped by what you said,
> ensnared by the words of your mouth,
> then do this, my son, to free yourself,
> since you have fallen into your neighbor's hands:
> Go and humble yourself;
> press your plea with your neighbor!
> Allow no sleep to your eyes,
> no slumber to your eyelids.
> Free yourself, like a gazelle from the hand of the hunter,
> like a bird from the snare of the fowler. (Prov. 6:1-5, NIV)

This passage is saying that the best way to lose a friend is to get into a shaky financial deal with him. How people change as soon as money comes on the scene! Someone has said that the best way to lose a friend is to lend him money or to sell him your used car.

> Do not make friends with a hot-tempered man,
> do not associate with one easily angered,
> or you may learn his ways
> and get yourself ensnared. (Prov. 22:24-25, NIV)

There's a lot of good common sense in the Bible, isn't there? This passage cautions us to be very careful about the friendships we make because they could have a severe impact on us.

Friendship makes certain demands on you—such as reciprocity, honesty, and loyalty. Reciprocity means having a relationship that is mutual, that flows two ways, that is accepting. Some people, observing the British scene, have said that the British pub is a very important part of British society. It is a place where absolutely anybody can go in and be accepted at face value, no questions asked. There is a certain degree of acceptance there for anyone.

Now obviously, this is the most superficial kind of relationship, but it reminds us of something important. Acceptance is a key to friendship. If my approach to a friendship is that I am going to correct somebody, that I am going to straighten out him or her, friendship is not going to grow out of the situation. There has to be a basic, mutual acceptance of what we are if friendship is to follow.

There also has to be a developing honesty between us, and loyalty, and commitment. All these things—reciprocity, honesty, and loyalty—are demanding. They are time consuming and, frankly, hard work at times. But if we want friends, we must be willing to work at it.

Once you have made a friendship, it is important to maintain it. There are four words that need to be emphasized in terms of maintaining friendships.

Caution

"A righteous man is cautious in friendship, but the way of the wicked leads them astray," says Proverbs 12:26 (NIV). Let us look at some ways in which caution in friendship is imperative. Note Proverbs 25:17: "Seldom set foot in your neighbor's house—too much of you, and he will hate you" (NIV).

When I was a teenager, I developed a close friendship with a young married couple who lived a few doors away. I hate to admit that the reason for this deep friendship was that they had gotten one of those newfangled things called a television. I became very friendly because of that. I remember my mother sitting me down and quoting Proverbs 25:17. That was good advice that I didn't want, but I learned to accept it eventually.

In maintaining friendships, beware of overkill. It is possible to become so smothering and demanding that you destroy the very thing you wanted to preserve.

If a man loudly blesses his neighbor early in the morning,
it will be taken as a curse. (Prov. 27:14, NIV)

Timing is everything. If you want to maintain a friendship, you don't call your friend at 4:00 A.M. to tell him what a neat guy he is. You use a little common sense.

Like one who takes away a garment on a cold day,
or like vinegar poured on soda,
is one who sings songs to a heavy heart. (Prov. 25:20, NIV)

I don't completely understand this verse, but I think it is saying that it is possible for us to be insensitive in our friendships. Often we don't take the trouble to find out how people are feeling. Instead, we transfer our feelings onto them. Here is this poor guy who has a heavy heart and his "friend" comes in all excited, slaps him on the back, punches him in the ribs, and says, "Hey, Buddy, it's great to be alive, isn't it?" "Buddy" replies, "No."

But the "friend" continues: "Oh come on, man, shake out of it. You're in great shape!" This kind of "friendship" is not needed at all.

Like a madman shooting
firebrands or deadly arrows
is a man who deceives his neighbor
and says, "I was only joking!" (Prov. 26:18-19, NIV)

Some people in their friendships begin to demonstrate a certain degree of insincerity. They needle and razz people, getting under their skin, until in the end those persons tell them to leave them alone.

"We were only kidding," they say. "Can't you take a joke?"

But no, they can't take a joke, because there is an element of meanness in this joking from these so-called friends. It is destructive and unkind. The jokers themselves have been insincere. We must guard against overkill, insensitivity, and insincerity if we are to maintain strong friendships.

Commitment

Third John is a very interesting letter. It is about the shortest book in the Bible, and over and over again in the fourteen verses is the term "dear friends." If you read this letter, you will get a very lovely picture. John, the aged apostle, writing to a group of believers, is pointing out that they are all his friends. He identifies in special ways some intimate friendships with the people there.

John is making a commitment to that fellowship of believers in general, and to individuals in the fellowship in particular, and so should we. There should be a degree to which you and I look in friendly terms toward the fellowship of believers. And when we do that, we should make a commitment to it. On the basis of the friendly commitment to the fellowship of believers, we should then be giving of ourselves in various ways so that we are building up "dear friend" relationships.

If we are to know fellowship and friendship, there has to be a commitment to the fellowship as a whole, and there has to be a readiness to identify individually with people for our good and for theirs. We need relationships. And they don't happen when we just come into church, sit among the people, and then go back home. Real friendships happen when there is commitment to the group as a whole, and when we get ourselves into situations where we can begin to nurture more personal, more intimate relationships.

Constancy

"Wealth brings many friends, but a poor man's friend deserts him," says Proverbs 19:4 (NIV). There is a kind of friendship that will last only until the weather changes.

At the moment of his betrayal, when Judas kissed him, Jesus said, "Friend, why have you come?" As far as Judas was concerned, that "friendship" could be discarded without much concern. This is like fair-weather friendships.

Constancy becomes especially difficult when we have passed the "comfort" stage of friendship and have begun to experience on a personal level the trials and struggles of our friends. Listening is hard and painful work when a friend is going through a death in the family, divorce, financial setbacks, or illness. True friends stay by our side when no one else is willing. And God gives grace, not only to the person going through the trial, but to the person being *a friend* to that person.

Candor

Finally, honesty, openness, "speaking the truth in love" is needed.

He who rebukes a man will in the end gain more favor than he who has a flattering tongue. (Prov. 28:23, NIV)

Genuine friendship requires honesty. But beware of the wrong kind of candor. "He who covers over an offense promotes love, but whoever repeats the matter separates close friends" (Prov. 17:9, NIV). And Proverbs 16:28 says, "A perverse man stirs up dissension, and a gossip separates close friends" (NIV).

To maintain a relationship, we need to know when to speak and when to keep silent; we need to know what to say and what not to say; we need to know to whom to speak and to whom not to speak. One of the quickest ways to destroy a friendship is through gossip. This is something we need to guard against. Unfortunately, in the church, what passes as candor and speaking the truth in love often is sheer, naked gossip, and it is destructive in the extreme.

What kind of friends do you have? And what kind of friend are you? Are you cautious, careful, committed, and candid? These are qualities we need to have. And what of the question I asked at the beginning? Are genuine friends luxuries or necessities? What do you think?

Let's Get Practical

1. What does it mean to be a friend of God's?

2. Why is genuine friendship a necessity?

3. Discuss the benefits of the following friendships:

   Men with men. Women with women

   Older people with younger people

   Men with women (nonromantic)

   People with their peers

4. How is genuine friendship costly to us? How does it benefit us?

5. What cautions must we take as we develop friendships?

6. How do commitment, candor, and constancy affect a friendship?

8

Employees: Called or Cursed?

If you and I sleep approximately eight hours, in a twenty-four hour period we are conscious for sixteen hours. If we work eight of those hours, we are spending half of our conscious hours at work. Therefore, it seems to me that we should be careful about our approach to work. I've observed that many people don't have good attitudes when it comes to work, and that may explain why they are having problems in their lives in general.

A man went on a construction site one day, and he stopped to ask one of the workers what he was doing. The laborer answered, "Do you see this pile of sand? I shovel it into this wheelbarrow and then push it over there, about seventy-five feet away. There I tip it over and make a new pile of sand. Then I come back for another load and do it all again. Probably by the time I have moved this sand over there, the boss will decide it is in the wrong place, and he'll tell me to take it someplace else."

Excusing himself, the visitor went to another worker and asked him what he was doing. And this man replied, "You've got to eat, haven't you? You've got to pay taxes, haven't you? The kids have got to have shoes for school, haven't they? I'm earning a living. That's why I'm here."

Now the visitor turned and walked a few feet, till he found a third man. And he asked him the same question: "What are you doing?"

"I am building a cathedral," came the answer.

"What do you mean, you're building a cathedral?"

"Well," the man answered, "that what's going on here. They've got a massive project underway. This whole site is going to be cleared. Very quickly we will start erecting a marvelous edifice, and I am excited. I am helping build a cathedral."

You can go to any place of work and find people who are merely "moving sand." You will find others who are simply earning a living. But you will also meet some people who have a vision of their work being something grander and greater than just shoveling sand or earning a living. To these people, work has significance.

Are Real Workers Cursed or Called?

Some people have the idea that work is a curse, while others look upon it as a calling. Depending upon which view you take, you are spending half of your conscious hours in a generally happy pursuit, or you are largely unfulfilled and unhappy.

With that in mind, I would like to direct your attention to the book of Ecclesiastes. It is descriptive, and certainly sounds as though it were written with the twentieth century in mind. The man who wrote Ecclesiastes was blessed with a healthy skepticism:

I thought in my heart, "Come now, I will test you with pleasure to find out what is good." But that also proved to be meaningless. "Laughter," I said, "is foolish. And what does pleasure accomplish?" I tried cheering myself with wine, and embracing folly—my mind still guiding me with wisdom. I wanted to see what was worthwhile for men to do under heaven during the few days of their lives.

I undertook great projects: I built houses for myself and planted vineyards. I made gardens and parks and planted all kinds of fruit trees in them. I made reservoirs to water groves of flourishing trees. I bought male and female slaves and had other slaves who were born in my house. I also owned more herds and flocks than anyone in Jerusalem before me. I amassed silver and gold for myself, and the treasure of kings and provinces. I acquired men and women singers, and a harem as well—the delights of the heart of man. I became greater by far than anyone in Jerusalem before me. In all this my wisdom stayed with me.

> I denied myself nothing my eyes desired;
> I refused my heart no pleasure.
> My heart took delight in all my work,
> and this was the reward for all my labor.
> Yet when I surveyed all that my hands had done
> and what I had toiled to achieve,
> everything was meaningless, a chasing after the wind;
> nothing was gained under the sun. (Eccles. 2:1-11, NIV)

That is one view of work. The writer of Ecclesiastes set down the experience of a worker who knows what it is to be highly successful in his work. But in the end, he is not sure it was worth all his sweat and labor.

I want to explore some common work situations and the attitudes that normally accompany them. As we look at some examples, we will encounter several different approaches to the world of work.

Wendell Workaholic

First of all, let me introduce Wendell Workaholic. He is, of course, very busy. He is something of a perfectionist. He feels that if a thing is worth doing, it is worth doing properly. And he has come to the conclusion that if you want anything done properly, you've got to do it yourself. He finds that a lot of people don't deliver; they don't come through on time. So he takes up the slack—more and more all the time.

Frankly, he has little use for our three divisions in the day—eight hours of work, eight hours of sleep, and eight hours of leisure. He gets four to five hours of sleep at night, and the rest of the time he works. As a result, his family relationships have suffered. His wife has had it. He doesn't really know the kids. He's introduced to them occasionally, but they are getting very discouraged about the whole thing.

It is difficult to know whether the family is breaking up because Wendell is a workaholic, or whether he is a workaholic because his family is breaking up. Poor Wendell could rationalize his behavior in that he is so unhappy he doesn't want to go home. He goes and goes and goes, and it is only matter of time until he has the heart attack—or the divorce—he is working on so assiduously.

Lenny Lazy

Lenny Lazy is full of stories. He goes around all the time, livening up the place and causing you to laugh. But he doesn't do anything productive; in fact, he's a nuisance, though he is fun to have around. Not only does he not produce anything himself; he is very disruptive to the work of other people.

People like Lenny, but he is lazy. They don't like him, of course, if anything needs to be done, because Lenny just doesn't produce. His favorite Bible verse says, "Here am I; send him."

Pavlov Paycheck

Pavlov is a refugee from Eastern Europe. He was not into collectivism; he did not like the way things were going in his native country. He felt very strongly that the individual ought to have more freedom. So when the Marxists took over, he got out and came to the land of the free and the home of the brave. He came to America because it was the land of opportunity.

He's a hard worker, and upwardly mobile. He produces. What matters to him is the bottom line, the paycheck, and he doesn't worry about anything else because he is just so happy to see that he made the right choice. He looks at what has happened in Eastern Europe and says to himself, *Boy, am I glad I got out of that disaster. Here I am; look what I have done with my life! I have really made something out of myself.*

Randy Ripoff

Another worker we should meet is Randy Ripoff. Randy has a very simple approach to life: He believes that everybody owes him something. He figures that whatever is available is his for the taking. If he needs office supplies, he helps himself. If he wants a bit of time off, he takes it. If he wants to leave work early, he does so. If he wants to goof off during the course of the day, he gives himself that privilege.

Randy has no sense of obligation to anybody. He is only obligated to himself. He doesn't care who gets ripped off in the process, just as long as Randy is okay.

Fran Frazzle

Then there is Fran Frazzle. Her husband walked out on her, leaving her with two small kids, and he hasn't paid child support for years. She had to get back into the work force, and she has a hard time meeting all her financial obligations. She is worried about the kids, because she can't be at home when they get out of school.

Her health is not good, but she can't take time off to see about it because she is afraid that her job might not be there when she comes back. Not only is she under economic duress; she feels terribly guilty about the breakdown of her marriage. She worries about what her ex-husband is up to, and the kids are driving her to distraction. Because she can't concentrate, she is really not doing a very good job at work. The boss has just called Fran in and said to her, "Shape up or ship out."

Buck Bossman

Buck Bossman is appropriately named. He will buck anything— particularly the boss. He sees management as the adversary, the devil incarnate. In his view, management is there to abuse him. His favorite and oft-quoted expression is, "When are they going to do something for the workers?"

He is always ready to lay down his tools. At the drop of a hat,

119

when any issue comes up, he is prepared to stop what he is doing and make a bigger issue out of it. He will push it to its illogical extreme and keep propounding things like: "Workers of the world, unite!" "You've nothing to lose but your chains." This man has been well schooled in certain approaches and is totally committed to bucking the boss wherever he is found.

Cuthbert Coronary

Cuthbert Coronary, meanwhile, holds down a management position and sits in on the board meetings at his firm. Cuthbert is working on his coronary. He is troubled. Productivity is down. The market is drying up. The bank is closing in. There is threat of a strike. The bills are mounting up. His "in" tray is overflowing. He gets to the office dreading his work, and he dreads it the whole time he is there. He just wishes he had bought stock in Maalox, because he is keeping them in business. He is absolutely worried sick.

When he came out of business school he was excited about his work. But that excitement is now gone, along with the thrill and challenge. Work is one overwhelming, overpowering situation now, and he is not sure how much longer he can go on.

Percy Plodder

Percy Plodder, however, is still there. Percy Plodder is from the old school. He still believes in an honest day's wage for an honest day's work. He is a member of a dying breed.

Percy figures that he can trust people to give him an honest day's pay, though he knows there is nothing he can do personally to guarantee that. He does know that there is a lot he can do about an honest day's work, and you can rely on Percy. However, he has a problem. Some people in the union are getting on his case because Percy produces way above the average. That puts everybody else in a bad light. They are telling Percy to back off. "You're overdoing it, and you're making it very difficult for everybody else. Anyway, they are not paying you what you are worth."

This look at workers may be skeptical and cynical, but I have observed that there is a lot of skepticism and cynicism in the work place. What I have outlined here in caricature isn't much different from what can be found in any place of work. Many workers are dissatisfied.

Daniel Yankelovich, is his interesting book *New Rules*, said this: "Symptoms of worker frustration were visible everywhere in absenteeism, tardiness, carelessness, indifference, high turnover, number of union grievances, slowdowns in the periods preceding collective bargaining, and even sabotage. Mostly worker frustration showed in poor product quality" (*New Rules* [New York: Random House, 1981], p. 43).

He goes on to say that in the late seventies the University of Michigan conducted a survey of workers in the United States and discovered that 27 percent of all workers feel so ashamed of the quality of their work that they would not buy the product they are producing.

What is the result of that? Plummeting productivity. And as a further result, there is all kinds of misery in management. I find, in the spiritual counseling I do, gross dissatisfaction in people's work relationships.

The Bible and Work

Now let's look at work from a scriptural perspective. If you turn to Genesis 1, you will find something that's quite obvious, very elementary, and therefore very often ignored.

That is, God works. God created the world in six days. It is not my purpose here to interpret that; I simply point to the statement that explains something very basic. God is a God of creation, and because he is a God of creation, things exist. The very fact that we exist is related to the truth that God has blessed work. He himself is involved in work.

We can see this in the Ten Commandments. "Six days shalt thou labor and do all thy work. . . . The seventh is the sabbath of the Lord thy God."

The second thing we notice is in Genesis 2, that work is mandated by God for people. God put man and woman in the Garden and commissioned them to till the ground and to oversee the animals. In other words, he put them to work. And this was before what we call the Fall. This pattern was part of the Creation ordinance, what God built into humanity's original experience.

Genesis 3, however, tells us the sad story of the Fall. Man and woman decided that they did not want to be dependent on God. Acting independently of him, they died in the truest sense of what it means to be human. God responded to their disobedience by saying, "Cursed is the ground because of you."

The Hebrew word for "man" is *adam*, which is also the name given to the first man, Adam. The Hebrew word for "ground" or "earth" is *adamah*. Obviously, there is a clear link between the two. Scripture teaches us that Adam was created from the *adamah*, the dust of the earth. We are made from the dust, and we return to the dust. And all the time, we are related to the earth. Without the earth and its productivity, we could not survive. That's how God made us. We are closely related to the world of which we are a part.

When we became independent of God, a wrench was thrown into the works. Man would continue to work the ground as he had originally been told to do, as a noble thing, but now work became painful, hard, dull, and boring. It required sweat. Now work was going to be a curse.

A lot of people today believe that work is a curse; work is something visited upon us in some way to punish us. They believe it is always going to be bad, always going to be dull, always going to be drudgery. But those who hold to such ideas are wrong.

First, we do not base our theology—or our lives—on the Fall. We base our theology and our lives on Creation. Work was not a curse originally. Work was something God engaged in and something he wanted us to involved in from the beginning.

Second, if we recognize that there is a curse on work as the result of the Fall, we also recognize that God in redemption is turning back the consequences of the Fall. In my experience of redemption, I see that all of the consequences of the Fall are being rolled back. Work is not a burden. It is not drudgery. It is not dull. Work is significant.

Third, God is deeply concerned when work becomes the means of people abusing one another. In Exodus 1, we find that the people of Israel were in Egypt and were grossly abused by their taskmasters. They had to work in very cruel, inhuman conditions, and God clearly stood on their side. The result was the magnificent exodus, God bringing his people out from their bondage.

Fourth, and perhaps most significantly for us, when our Lord Jesus came into the world, he was born in humble circumstances. He lived in a town everybody despised and took a menial job, and for thirty years he worked in obscurity as a carpenter. His hands were calloused. He fixed plows and built tables for people. He did all the chores that needed to be done around the home.

It is hard for us to imagine that the one who came from eternity inhabited our world for thirty-three years and spent thirty of those years in obscurity. If ever God tried to communicate to us that there is something noble and honorable about work, it is hard to imagine how he could have done it more emphatically than he did in Jesus. Do you remember that at the end of his life, the Lord Jesus said, "I have finished the work that you gave me to do"? Scripture, therefore, has some powerful, positive things to say about work.

Work As Self-Fulfillment

Yankelovich, in *New Rules,* gives names to the trends within American society. He says that we used to live lives of self-denial. Sacrifice and hard work were regarded as honorable. But then things changed. Instead of self-denial being the basis of our work, we adopted the attitude of self-fulfillment. If one's work required more denial of self than he or she wanted to give, then one's duty to self was to get out of that job and find something more pleasant, more gratifying to self.

Yankelovich goes on to say that in a revolution, the first stage is to throw out everything—the "baby with the bathwater." The second stage of the revolution is to try to get the baby back in. Now, he says, we have begun to discover that self-fulfillment or duty to self leads to self-indulgence, and self-indulgence leads to hedonism, and hedonism leads inevitably to the destruction of the individual and of society. So, he says, we are trying to blend self-denial and self-fulfillment. Amen! Isn't it exciting to see how we eventually get back to what the Bible has been saying all along? If we wait long enough, it is amazing how people begin to see that the old way they once despised is really the only way.

The Bible clearly teaches that self-fulfillment is a very significant aspect of our lives. Why? Well, first of all, God made each of us unique. He wants us to fulfill all that he has in mind uniquely for us.

This fact of uniqueness is related to our godlikeness. You are not an animal. You are not a vegetable, nor a mineral; you are a person. What is it about you as a person that makes you different from the animals, or vegetables, or minerals? God said that being made in the image of God is what makes us different. One aspect of godlikeness or being made in the image of God is this: The Creator created us to be creative. We have to use the word *creative* carefully, of course. God did not make us to be as creative as he is, for he created the world out of nothing. He doesn't expect us to create things out of nothing. But he does expect us to take the raw materials he has given us and to create with them.

To the degree that we create, we demonstrate the uniqueness of our humanity. Creativity means work. Therefore, in a very real sense, my work and the way I go about it will determine my creativity, and my creativity will determine to a large extent how far I fulfill that for which I was created.

Not only are we unique; the Bible teaches that everybody is gifted. Each person possesses certain skills. We are also gifted with time, and with energy.

We cannot create our skills. But we can hone them, develop them, and be trained in their use. We cannot create time. We cannot manufacture energy. But we can use or abuse them both. God gives us skills, along with the time and energy to manage them. These are gracious gifts from our heavenly Father. What a privilege to wake up in the morning and to know that the skills God has given me are there. The time he wants me to have is available to me, and the energy that I need for the tasks he has in mind for me—that will be mine. I embark on the day, transferring these glorious gifts into the purposes for which I was created and for which I have been redeemed.

How do I translate these gifts into the purposes for which God ordained me? By work. By doing something, achieving something, producing something.

If this is true, then my completeness as a person—my sense of fulfillment—is going to be related to my productivity. What I am producing in my life is going to be a demonstration of my giftedness, my uniqueness, and my humanness.

I feel that one of the tragedies in our society now is that people think they will find self-fulfillment by turning away from honest, productive, creative, hard work. On the contrary, it is in their commitment to creative, productive work that they are most likely to find the fulfillment they seek. The Bible clearly teaches that man and woman are going to be the most fulfilled when they are doing what they were uniquely created to do.

Work and Our Society

We have seen what the Bible says about work. And we have considered the truth that work is to bring us self-fulfillment. There is also a social aspect to work. The Bible teaches us, and we are all aware of it, that we do not live our lives in isolation. How we relate to our society is a very important factor in terms of our enjoyment of life.

The Lord Jesus had something to say about this. He said, in effect, "Listen, you are a part of society, and you serve the society of which you are a part." That meant that on one occasion when he and his disciples entered a house and were not given the common courtesy of foot washing, the Lord Jesus washed their feet. The disciples evidently considered that it was menial labor, women's work, a slave's work, and that since they were men, they weren't going to do it. But Jesus took off his outer garment, got a towel and a basin, and washed their feet. He then sat down and, having got their attention, explained to them the example he had given them (see John 13).

The example was very basic: They were not to have the attitude that they were to be served; they were present in order to serve others.

He repeated it at other times. "I am your Master and Lord," he said. "I didn't come to be served, but to serve. If you are my servants, therefore, that should be your attitude." The believer not only believes in being fulfilled through work because that is what he is created to do; the believer also knows that he owes a debt to society—that he has a responsibility and that he should be producing something through his creativity that will benefit the society of which he is a part.

This is a part of what the Bible teaches about work. So I need to check on my acceptance or rejection of scriptural principles of work, and to determine whether my life is truly being fulfilled. Am I doing the work that God has uniquely planned for me? Am I engaging in work that can be said to be benefiting society?

Work from a Spiritual Perspective

An old Latin axiom says: *Orare est laborare. Laborare est orare. Orare* means "to worship or pray." That is the word from which we get such terms as *oration* or *oratory. Laborare* means "to work." Obviously, we get our word *labor* from this word. The saying means, simply, "To worship is to work; to work is to worship."

First let's consider the initial phrase—"to worship is to work." When you go to a worship service, do you go ready to work? Or do you say to yourself, *Sunday is my day off. I don't do anything. The minister works Sundays, not me*. I suggest to you that this approach misses the point of worship. Worship is work. You and I go to worship service committing ourselves to working with our minds, our lungs, and our voices, to engage ourselves in identifying with the God whom we love and whom we serve. To worship is to work.

But we are particularly interested in this remarkable idea: To work is to worship.

Work Is a Calling from God

What the second phrase of that saying means is that Christians look at work from a spiritual perspective. We have the idea that our work is not merely a drudgery we must attend to, but a task to which God calls us. In medieval Christianity, the predominant idea was that God called certain people—and *their* work was a "calling." The rest of the people just worked. That was how we got this awful division between the clergy and the laity; the clergy were called, the laity just got on with it. This attitude was very common. A few people received a high calling into the priesthood, and the rest of the folk just went through the sheer drudgery of their work.

Then along came the Reformation, in which one or two ancient biblical doctrines were rediscovered, including the priesthood of all believers. All believers in Jesus Christ are one in Christ Jesus, and we are all "a kingdom of priests" (1 Pet. 2:5, 9). All of us have immediate access to the Father through the Son, and we don't need to go through a priest or any other human agent.

What other truth does this idea lead us to? *If everybody is a priest before God, everybody is equally called.* And if everybody is equally called, then the work you are in—if God wants you in it—is your calling.

We might answer: "Come on. I'm just an electrician," or "I'm just a homemaker," or "But I work in a multimillion-dollar industry that has nothing to do with God or religion!" We are used to seeing life divided in this way. But in God's eyes there's no such thing as "just a homemaker." You can rule out "just a" when you talk about your job, if you believe that work is a calling. Paul suggests in 1 Corinthians 7:20 that the work you are involved in is as much a divine calling as that in which a missionary or a pastor is involved. This means that "nonreligious" jobs can also be callings. Of course we are aware of some livelihoods that work against God's kingdom by their very nature, and any type of work that is against God cannot be work to which a Christian is called. But if Christians were not called into secular work places, how would Christianity's positive impact ever be felt in those situations? If we believe that we are called to the work that is before us, I will guarantee a positive shift of attitude toward that work.

When you check into work tomorrow morning, say to the Lord, *Here I am, Lord, uniquely gifted with skill, time, and energy that you have graciously provided. I recognize this. And I believe that you have me where you want me, which means that this particular job that I thought last week was a real bummer is, in actual fact, a high calling. And I am going to live and work today as if that is exactly what it is.*

Work Is Cooperation with God

Not only is work a calling; it is cooperation. When God said to Adam and Eve in the beginning to till the garden, what he was really saying was, "Let's cooperate." Paul picks up on the same idea. He says that we are "workers together with God" (1 Cor. 3:9). God's Word is saying that one of the high and noble privileges of being a human being is that we are called to cooperate with God in the work that is going on in the universe.

A preacher visited a farmer one day. Standing on a hill, looking over the farm, they beheld a beautiful field of corn. It was a great crop—lovely, long, straight lines; tall, green shoots; large ears of corn all ready to be picked. As the preacher looked at it, he was rejoicing. "Oh," he said, "the Lord has blessed you magnificently! Just look how the Lord has sent the rain and has given you the soil, the seed, and the increase! Isn't the Lord wonderful? I am sure that when you come out here to work every morning you just praise the Lord, don't you?"

The old farmer answered, "Yes, I do. But you should have seen what it was like when he had it on his own."

When the Lord had it "on his own," the soil and the rain and the miracle of increase were all working, but the place was a jungle, a wilderness. Those have their place, but they are not very good for growing corn. If you are going to grow corn to feed people, then you need a farmer. But the farmer can't invent the soil, create rain, or perform the miracle of reproduction. God does that.

The farmer is superb at plowing and planting straight rows. And he can invent all kinds of machinery that can harvest the corn and market it. Work is cooperation with God.

If you can begin to think of work first of all as a calling and then as cooperation, you can begin to think of it in a very real sense as worship. *Laborare est orare.*

Work Is Caring on Behalf of God

The Bible teaches us that we work in order that we might produce. We produce in order that we might provide. The Bible says that the man who does not provide for his own family is worse than an unbeliever and has denied the faith. But the persons who do produce and therefore provide are demonstrating personal care for the family. And as they do that, they are doing something of profound significance. There is a very real sense in which they are honoring the Lord in their work. Not only that, but the Scripture tells us that those who have stolen as a past lifestyle should stop stealing. In the future, they should work with their hands that which is good in order that they might have enough to share with those in need.

We work to produce, in order that we might provide, not only for our own families, but also for those in need. As we begin to care for those who are in need around us, we are honoring the Lord. To work is to worship.

Work Is Coming to God

There is an aspect of work that is in fact an offering of ourselves to God. When we work, we produce. And what we produce is very much a part of us.

Jill and I have one or two original paintings in our home. They are some of our most treasured possessions. This is because they were given to us by the artists as expressions of appreciation. The artists say we ministered to them and that is why they have done this. These paintings are an extension of the artists who gave them to us. They were brought into being because of unique gifts and abilities.

Likewise, when you create something and turn it into money, that money or wealth is a projection of you. That's why from the beginning of time, men and women have been encouraged to see that what they produce is an extension of themselves, and they bring part of that to God as tangible evidence of their relationship to him. One of the great things about working is that it equips you to bring an offering to the Lord. When you bring such an offering to the Lord, you are bringing yourself to him.

The Scripture taught this from the beginning. Old Testament law set forth a system called tithing. Each Israelite was to give a tenth of his income to the Lord. (If you study the pertinent Scriptures carefully, you will see that it was closer to 25 percent of their income. The tenth was set aside specifically for the work of the Lord.) Some people transfer that into the New Testament and teach that believers should be giving a tenth of their income to the Lord. The principle that we give in relation to the way the Lord has provided for us is quite clear in the New Testament.

We need to understand that when we work and produce, this offering is an extension of ourselves. If we want to demonstrate to the Lord how much we love him, we give ourselves to him. One of the best ways to do that is to give that which speaks so forcefully of ourselves—that which we have created or produced.

Are you giving to the Lord? The Bible says that the Lord loves a cheerful giver—the word in the Greek actually could mean a "hilarious" giver. Wouldn't it be great if, when the offering plate was passed in your church, the people were doubling up with the fun and hilarity of giving?

Problems of Work, Unemployment, and Retirement

Many problems in the work place are related directly to management. One of the best antidotes for management problems, as far as the Christian manager is concerned, is to take seriously Colossians 4:1. This verse reminds the boss that *he* has a boss. He has a Master who is sitting in heaven, keeping his accounts. Knowing that would clear up a lot of problems, if managers believed it.

There's also the issue of adjustments in employment. A lot of people need to take another look at their employment situations. We should ask ourselves some basic questions:

- Why am I doing what I am doing?
- What is my attitude toward what I am doing?
- Do I continually find myself challenged in my place of employment, in light of all that Scripture says about work?
- Am I doing what I feel that God really wants me to do?

If you are where God wants you, enjoy it. If you need to change employment, ask yourself why you are contemplating a change. What are the factors leading to it, and how do they match what we have discussed about the Christian's approach to work?

What about unemployment? As I write this, 8.4 million people in the United States are officially unemployed. In addition, two or three million have stopped looking. As a nation, probably twelve million are out of work. Some are out of work because they want to be; others are out of work because they can't find work. What should our attitude be?

To be out of work but not seeking employment is simply an unacceptable approach to the situation. A total of $31.5 billion was paid out in 1983 in unemployment benefits in the United States. Somebody has got to earn that. The person who chooses not to work and lives off everybody else is a parasite, and that is flatly contradictory to Christian principles.

What about those who are unemployed and would give anything to find a job? We have got to recognize the policies that are producing unemployment and decide what we believe about these policies. As Christians who are a part of society, we have got to do what we can to rectify those policies. We've got to take a hard look at what is going on in our country, meanwhile encouraging those who would love to work and can't find the opportunity to do so. The church is a primary place—or should be—where the unemployed can find encouragement and in some cases a lead to a job. This kind of networking is part of the beauty of community, particularly among God's people.

Finally, what about retirement? A lot of people can't wait to retire. To do what? To lie in a hammock, drink cool drinks, and play golf? To travel to Florida or Arizona as quickly as possible? Is that what retirement is for?

If you were to do a Bible study on retirement, you wouldn't need a notebook, because the Bible does not address this modern issue.

Retirement should not be about the ceasing of work, because people were created to be productive. Retirement should be a season in which a person has a new liberty to engage in a different kind of service. We should be honoring the Lord, benefiting society, and finding fulfillment until the day we die. Christians need to evaluate the concept of retirement in light of God's ultimate purposes for people.

My hope is that we would have a genuinely Christian view of work, that we would honestly be able to say, "To work is to worship"—and that we would respond to what the apostle said when he wrote:

Whatever you do, do it heartily as unto the Lord, for you serve the Lord Christ.

Let's Get Practical

1. Discuss the scriptural basis for work.

2. Which of the character profiles described on pages 117–120 most closely fit your attitude toward work? How might you improve your own attitude toward and/or performance at work?

3. How can work be fulfilling to us, even if it isn't a great job or a formal ministry?

4. How or why has work been a worship experience for you? If it has not been, how might it become more worshipful?

5. Discuss these aspects of work, concerning our relationship with God.

    calling from God:

    cooperation with God:

    caring on behalf of God:

    coming to God:

6. How can we reconcile unemployment, underemployment, or unsuitable employment with what we know about God's purposes for our work?

9

The Family That Stays Together

They used to say, "The family that prays together stays together." But then they discovered that a lot of families don't like praying very much. So they changed the saying slightly to "The family that plays together stays together." I think probably we're going to have to change it again, because it seems that fewer and fewer families are staying together.

Scripture makes it very clear that God's basic societal unit is the family, and it is obvious that the family is intended to be an environment of great delight. But far from being an environment of great delight, the family too often is the scene of intolerable stress and strain.

We can find basic principles for family living in Scripture, and in this chapter we will consider some that we should respect and adhere to. But I personally don't think there are any absolute guarantees for creating or maintaining happy family life. I know of families where the parents seem to do everything right, and they breed a bunch of rascals. I know of families that seem to do everything wrong, but the kids have turned out to be remarkable people. The reason for this, of course, is that every individual is a person who makes his or her own choices. The family can direct the way that the choices *should* be made, but the individual has the responsibility and the freedom to make the choices in the end. And so, while there is much that we can build into our families, we have to recognize that the individual choices are going to determine the way people go in the end.

Our reference point in this chapter is the story of Isaac, in Genesis 25:21-34. By looking into this account, I want to try to answer three questions: How are families founded? Why do families fail? And when do families flourish?

How Are Real Families Founded?

If we're going to have a real family we have to make sure that we base it properly, so we need to ask, How are families founded?

As far as the story of Isaac is concerned, we have considerable detail as to the answer. You remember that God had spoken to Isaac's father, Abraham, and had told him that through him would come blessing for the whole world. The problem was that when the promise was given to Abraham, he was seventy-five and his wife was only ten years younger. They had not been able to have a child when they were young, so the chances of progeny were remote. However, eventually little Isaac came along. It was so amazing, so hilarious, so hysterical, that Abraham and Sarah named the baby *Isaac*, which means "laughter."

When Isaac was born, Abraham was a hundred years of age. So when Isaac grew up and was ready to marry, Abraham was very, very old. But Abraham had to make sure that the line of succession through Isaac was continued, the heritage of blessing that God had promised. A wife was needed, and a careful choice had to be made. So Abraham did what was customary in those times. He called his trusted servant, probably Eliezer, and told him to go and find a wife for Isaac.

That was a slightly different approach from the way we do it today. It would be like a dad deciding that one of the fellows down at the factory or office should pick out a wife for his son.

Eliezer was told to make sure that he didn't take a wife from the immediate surroundings. "Don't get a wife from the Canaanites," Abraham commanded. What the Canaanites stood for morally and religiously was totally abhorrent to God. "No, go back to our own people, and there find a wife for my son Isaac."

Eliezer asked, "What if she doesn't want to be uprooted from where she is living and come with me?" And the answer was, if she did not want to come with him, he should forget it. He would be released from his oath. And again Abraham told him that a wife for Isaac must not be taken from among the Canaanites.

Eliezer went off with those instructions. He was a man of prayer, and according to the account in Genesis 24, he repeatedly prayed that he might make the right choice. He was also the sort of person who looked for specific guidance. So he asked the Lord, "When I get to the right place, how will I know which girl to pick? Do I pick the cutest? the smartest? the wealthiest? What do I do? I'm going to need help." As they communed together, God and this servant of Abraham, Eliezer was led to ask the Lord for specific help. He said, "Would you let it be that when I ask her for a drink of water, as I sit by the well, that she'll give me a drink and water my camels as well?"

That doesn't seem like much to us, but a camel can drink twenty-five gallons of water at one time. And this man had ten of them. She had to draw two hundred and fifty gallons of water out of this well, one bucket at a time, on the end of a rope? She was some lady, I guess, to be able to water all those camels. I have been in the desert and watched people watering camels. It's always the women who do it. The men sit under the palm trees discussing "important business," while the women water the camels. It takes hours to do it. And so to say, "Sure, and I'll water your camels," she would have to be somebody unusual.

Rebekah came to the well, and Eliezer asked her for a drink, as he said he would. And Rebekah not only gave him a drink; she watered his camels as well. He told her what his business was, and she returned to her home and discussed it with the family. The family agreed that she should go and marry Isaac. Then the question was put to her: "Will you go with this man?" And she said, "I will." So they put her on a camel, and away she went to marry a man she had never seen.

When the camels came near Isaac's home, he was out in the field "meditating," the Scripture says. Their approach is slightly different from what's common today. In those days, a man would marry, and then he would take his bride into his tent. Only then would he lift up her veil. And he would either faint or cry, "Yippee!" It all depended on what sort of girl he got. As far as Rebekah was concerned, she was absolutely magnificent. The Scriptures say that she was beautiful, which certainly helps; she was a virgin, which was necessary; and she was willing to go. These were her characteristics. So she came to Isaac, and that's how this family was founded. It got off to a superb start.

Now let's consider one or two lessons from this. How are families founded?

Marriages made with care

In England we have an expression, "Marry in haste; repent at leisure." And I have seen this happen over, and over, and over again.

If you are contemplating marriage, take your time. You are married a long time and have lots of time to regret a wrong decision. Make sure that your marriage is made with care.

How do you do that? First of all, according to this story, there are clearly defined principles. The Bible teaches, in the same way that Abraham's son was not to marry a Canaanite woman, a believer should not marry an unbeliever. That is unequivocal.

Frequently people will say to me, "Would you perform our marriage ceremony?" And I answer, "Well, let's talk about it."

They look mildly aghast: "Talk about it? What is there to talk about?" If I am to officiate at a wedding, I want, before the Lord, to be proud of the coming marriage. God is going to join two people together, and I'm going to be, in some way, involved in that unique thing God is doing.

I want to talk to them about the spiritual basis of their relationship, what the man understands about the Lord, and what the woman understands about the Lord. I want to find out if they have a unanimity, a oneness, a spiritual mutuality between them. That is a principle of Christian marriage.

I am not suggesting that healthy marriages are not possible between people who aren't believers; of course they are. Neither am I suggesting that believers cannot have unhealthy marriages. We all know to our pain and shame that believers can have poor marriages. What I am saying is that if we are going to marry according to divine principle, believers will marry believers. And this doesn't mean that a prospective mate qualifies because he has made a profession of faith in Christ or because she comes to church with the believer once in a while. "You know," I am told by the young girl who begs me to perform her ceremony, "he's not too enthusiastic, but . . . yes . . . I think he believes."

I am not talking about that sort of "hope-so" spiritual union. If you want to found a Christian family, you found it on a marriage of two believers committed to each other and joined together by the Lord. These believers go about marriage on the basis of obedience to the commands of God, as did Isaac and Rebekah, on the basis of God's guidance that was made available to them.

How does a person get guidance? How do you find out what God wants you to do? Some people say, "I lay out a fleece, like Gideon did, or like Eliezer. If a young lady comes and offers to water my camels, she's got to be the one."

Rebekah certainly was unusual to do what she did, as we've pointed out. But sometimes we can ask for signs and the signs will come up just the way we want them, because we ask for things that we are fairly sure of anyway. We may find that the sign comes, but that it's all wrong.

Some say, "Well, I have peace about this." And the criterion upon which they base their decision is that they "have peace." I've met people who are totally at peace while being blatantly disobedient. We can chloroform our conscience without too much trouble. Jonah is an example of this. God told him to go to Nineveh, but he decided to go to Tarshish, which was as far as he could go in the opposite direction. He found a ship at the seacoast, and it was destined for Tarshish. Maybe he told himself, *It must be right. There's a ship going there.*

He found a berth on the ship. *It must be right,* he again persuaded himself. *There's a berth for me.* He purchased his ticket. *I have the right amount of money; it must be right.*

You see, everything fit beautifully into place to allow Jonah to be flatly disobedient. And he had peace about it. We know that, because he fell asleep in the story. To do that, you've got to be at peace.

So we cannot make our determinations merely by "fleeces," nor by peace, for fleece and peace can simply mean that we are allowing factors to come in to cover what God has told us is not right. If, on the other hand, we are prepared to obey God's command and are committed to knowing his will, we can build a marriage made with care.

In Isaac and Rebekah's marriage, there was a *clearly stated commitment.* The question addressed to this young lady was, "Will you go with this man?" And she said, "I will." This commitment was challenging. It was demanding. She understood what she was doing, and she made her choice freely. Make no mistake about it; marriage is made with care, and it is based on a clearly stated commitment. It is "for richer or for poorer, in sickness and in health . . . till death us do part." That is the principle God has ordained. It is a challenge we face, a commitment we make.

We also see in Isaac and Rebekah's marriage that there was *clearly expressed love.* Isaac was meditating in the field, and somebody said, "The camels are coming." He looked, and sitting on one of the camels was a lady draped in a veil. He had no idea what sort of bride he was going to get, but she was presented to him, and very shortly the story says, "Isaac loved his wife."

He did not choose her on the basis of her physical beauty. They had no basis for infatuation. There were none of the things that so often go into the dating game, which becomes the marriage game, which often finishes up as the divorce game. None of these factors had much part in their marriage.

This marriage was built on the basis of God's guidance, God's commands, mature advice, and sensible, sound decisions.

I'm not suggesting that we go back to the patriarchal system. But if young people are going to marry, they'd better make sure that they're prepared to do it on the basis of knowing God's will, obeying God's commands, following God's guidance, and seeking all the help and guidance they can get from people who have years of experience—people of profound spiritual insight. When they begin to do this, they can begin to respond to each other with the kind of love that is not only romantic, sentimental, or sexual, but which is committed. Remember, love is not a feeling. Love is a commitment. This was the basis of Isaac and Rebekah's marriage.

When you see how these two prepared for their marriage, the prognosis could reasonably be: This will be a superb family. Well, let's read on and see what happened.

Children bathed in prayer

Not only was this marriage made with care, but its children were bathed in prayer. These two little ideas are important, and they are easy to remember: Marriage made with care; children bathed in prayer.

People are deciding to have children now for a variety of reasons. Many single women are deciding to have children because they feel unfulfilled without them. That is a desperately selfish approach. Some people have children whom they use as a weapon against their former spouse. The children are being abused in all kinds of ways in these relationships.

When we think of children from a biblical viewpoint, we've got to think like Isaac did. We pray for our children because we understand that children are on loan from the Lord. They're not given to us for our own fulfillment—although our fulfillment often occurs in the process of being a parent. Children are given to us that we might be the means of bringing into this world persons who will last for eternity. Parents are not owners of their children; they never were, and they never will be. Parents are stewards of their children;

they are bringing them up before the Lord for the Lord's ultimate purposes.

When a man and a woman begin to pray for their offspring even before they are born, when the child is actually born and they give thanks to the Lord and commit the child to him, they show that deep down in their hearts they know what is going on. They know that God is the giver of this new life. They are beginning to build the basis of a solid family.

You may be thinking, *I wish I had known this a few years ago. I didn't get into marriage like this, and we didn't have our kids like this either.* Some people don't make a very good start, but they make a superb finish. Others begin with a superb start, but they never finish. In the Dream Mile race in Oslo recently, two half-milers were entered for the purpose of setting a fast pace, so that a world record would result. Those two made a superb start, but they only lasted two laps. Some people start off in marriage like that, and then they peter out, while others begin badly and finish well. How we finish is infinitely more important than how we start. The sensible thing to do is to start a family God's way, and keep it up.

Remember: Marriage made with care; children bathed in prayer. As far as Isaac and Rebekah's children were concerned, they had a good start. They were bathed in prayer.

Isaac prayed for his children before they were a gleam in his eye. Isaac prayed that children would come because he had a tremendous sense of the purposes of God in the birth of children.

Rebekah prayed as well. When she finally became pregnant, she soon realized that a battle was starting inside her womb. She would have welcomed morning sickness; it would have been a relief from the discomfort she now experienced. The twins inside her womb would spend the whole of their lives fighting, and they were practicing inside her. In the end she prayed, "Why me? Why do I have to have twins like this?"

The Lord answered, "Two nations are in your womb. Two peoples from within you will be separated. One people will be stronger than the other, and the older will serve the younger." Through prayer, Rebekah gained insight from God about her children.

Why Do Families Fail?

As far as Isaac and Rebekah's family is concerned, all kinds of things went wrong. We can profit from their troubles if we look at their situation carefully and ask some important questions.

What constitutes failure? Two things become very evident in this story. First, there was an atmosphere of intrigue. And secondly, there was an atmosphere of indifference.

Intrigue

God had said to Rebekah and to Isaac that twins were to be born, and that the seed of Abraham would continue. The covenant purposes were right on track. But God told them an interesting thing: The younger one would be the one through whom the promised line would be perpetuated. That was abnormal. Usually the elder son inherited the family name and the blessing. But on this occasion it would be the younger one.

Isaac and Rebekah could have accepted what God said. The boys could have been told right from the beginning that this was to be the plan, since God had said that the younger would rule the elder. But for some reason, nobody accepted it. Isaac tried to give the best things to the older son. Rebekah decided that she would have to connive to see that Jacob, the younger of the two, got the best things. Esau couldn't care less about who got the blessing— until it was too late. And Jacob decided that he had to rip his brother off. So, a bad, bad scene developed.

One day Jacob, who often stayed home with his mother, was making stew when Esau came home. "Red," as his nickname could have been, had been hunting, and he was famished. He said, "Hey! Give me some of that stew."

Smooth, cunning Jacob said, "Sell me your birthright first."

Esau was so hungry he was about to die. *What good is a birthright if I keel over dead?* he said to himself. "Give me the stew." So he exchanged his birthright for a dish of stew.

To possess the birthright meant that Jacob was now the elder son. Profound responsibility and considerable honor went with this position. The one with the birthright would get twice the resources of the other brother to enable him to fulfill his responsibility.

Their mother, who was behind all of this, was on Jacob's side. And old Isaac, he didn't much care. In that way he was like Esau.

All kinds of trouble were brewing. Mother was behind Jacob, conniving and scheming. And Esau and Isaac were in each other's pockets, doing their own thing. All of them were careless about spiritual things; God's plan seemed to be forgotten. The problem was this: Instead of the family being one, they had chosen sides against one another. No one was telling the truth. There was a lot of scheming, instead of mutual support. There was a lot of lying instead of loving; and there was confusion instead of concern.

We can see those same things in families, and they indicate the demise of those families unless the problems are addressed very quickly.

Indifference

Note the attitude of indifference in the family of Isaac and Rebekah. Old man Isaac was becoming infirm. He figured that he was going to die, and he now had to bless his sons. He was intent on blessing the older son, Esau, even though he knew that God had chosen Jacob and that the birthright had been sold and an oath had been made. Even though he knew all this, he was still intent on doing it in the way that God didn't want it done.

Meanwhile, the wife was intent on getting the blessing her way. What she and Jacob did shows total indifference to the old man's infirmity, because they attacked him in all the areas in which he was weak.

His sight was going, so they knew that he couldn't recognize which son came into his room. His sense of smell had gone, so he couldn't tell the difference between roast goat and venison, which he loved for Esau to prepare for him.

Jacob went in to see his father—Jacob was smooth and Esau was hairy—and his smooth arms were covered with the skin of a goat.

Isaac called him to come near so that he could feel him, for Jacob's voice didn't quite sound like Esau's to him. He rubbed his hands on Jacob's arms and couldn't tell the difference between a hairy arm and the skin of a dead goat. His sense of touch had gone; he thought Jacob was Esau.

Isaac's sight was gone; his hearing was almost gone; his sense of touch was gone! And everybody was indifferent. Rebekah and Jacob saw his weakness as something on which they could capitalize.

There was also indifference to the young men's limitations. Esau obviously had his limitations. Would it not have been good if someone had said to Esau, "You are a great kid for sport, for hunting and fishing and having a good time, but you have some deficiencies in this other area." Would it not have been great if someone had said to Jacob, "Boy, you are so smart. But you are too smart for your own good. If you are not careful, you are going to use those wits of yours to rip people off and get yourself in all kinds of trouble." Would it not have been good if someone had sat down and helped the kids? But there was total indifference. "Let them do what they want," was the attitude.

Have you ever seen indifference to a young person's limitations? Have you ever seen indifference to an old person's infirmities? Have you ever seen indifference to matters of integrity in a family? When you do, be warned. The family is failing.

What are the causes of this family's failure?

As far as the father was concerned, he needed to accept some of the responsibility. One thing that's quite obvious about Isaac is that regardless of the superb start he made in life, he had come to disregard divine revelation. He was disinterested in what God had to say. He trusted normal, natural criteria, and they fooled him. He knew that an oath had been taken, but he said, "Who cares about oaths?" And as far as his sons were concerned, instead of handling them evenly, there was marked prejudice in his treatment; he favored one over the other.

When a father begins to disregard important things, and depends on the wrong things—when he begins to display an unbalanced, prejudicial attitude toward his children—he has to accept the major share of the responsibility for the family's failure.

I say to fathers: Listen, Dad. There never was such a thing as a perfect father who never made a mistake. If you have children, have you ever sat your first one down and said, "Sorry, kid; we were practicing on you. We had never had one before. If only somebody could have loaned us a kid to learn on first. . . . We figured we had just gotten you sorted out when you did a weird thing; you changed into an adolescent. We had never had one of those, either. And then you degenerated into a teenager! And all sorts of strange things happened to you. We were learning on you."

Of course, there never was a perfect father. But there can be fathers who are honest before God, honest with their children, and honest with their wives, who say, "There are some things around here that I need help with. I have become so materialistic, so naturalistic in my outlook, that I have not been a leader where divine principles are concerned. I have become so wrapped up in so many things that I have not even been interested in your spiritual or physical well-being. I have left it to someone else." A father can be honest and take a more responsible attitude.

What about the mother? Rebekah started off beautifully, but she became dedicated to her own ends. She knew what she wanted, and she knew how she was going to get it. As far as she was concerned, no stone should lie unturned; the ends justified the means. She was operating exclusively to her own advantage. She had no compunction whatsoever in humiliating her husband, and when her sons came on the scene, it was rank, crass manipulation all of the time. I don't know what happened to Rebekah, but when there is a conniving, scheming, manipulating woman in the family, who uses her husband and kids to get her own ends, you have got problems in the family.

We don't need to look far to see why this family failed. What can be said about there being no such thing as a perfect father obviously pertains to the mother also. What about the sons? Well, they were beauties. Esau lacked any sense of priority. As far as he was concerned, give him his bows and arrows and his hunting license and he was satisfied—and make sure there is plenty to eat when he gets home. Jacob lacked any sense of principle. He had learned well at his mother's knee how to connive and scheme. There are two boys here—one who lacks any sense of priority and one who lacks any sense of principle. The father has given up on everything, and the mother is manipulating all of them. In this family we see a recipe for disaster.

When Do Families Flourish?

Turning to a happier point, when do families flourish? Families flourish, I believe, when these ingredients are persistently and consistently mixed into the relationships: the father acts as head, the mother is supportive, the children are respectful, the family affirms itself, and the Lord adds his blessing.

The father acts as head

What do I mean by that? When I talk of father being the "head" of the family, I am not talking about the old patriarchal system where Father sits at one end of the table, bangs his fist, and says, "Do this. Don't do that," and when he is asked timorously by somebody in the family, "Why, Dad?" he says, "because I said so." That is not leadership. That is tyranny.

When we talk about the "head" in Scripture, we are talking about headship similar to the headship of Christ and his church. When we think of Christ's headship of his church, we discover, especially in Ephesians 5, that it certainly speaks of authority. But it speaks of nourishing, caring, providing, overshadowing, overseeing; it speaks of a tremendous sense of responsibility for caring for, nurturing, encouraging, and building up. If a family is going to flourish, fathers must commit themselves to caring for the mother and the children and giving of themselves to bring the children up the way that God wants them brought up. That is what headship means.

The mother is supportive

What does Mother do? Mother says, "Amen. I'm with you; I totally agree," and gives her support.

There is no sense of superiority or inferiority in this relationship. The creation principle in Scripture is abundantly clear, showing a mutuality and equality of the sexes. In redemption, Scripture takes great pains to show that in Christ there is neither male nor female. The apostle Paul is careful to point out that the principle of submission means mutual submission as unto the Lord. There is no suggestion of inferiority or superiority; it is simply a mutuality of experience, with father accepting his privileged sense of responsibility, knowing that he can count on a resource that is totally supportive.

This doesn't mean that to whatever he says the mother obediently replies, "Yes, my dear; very good, dear." It does not imply a cringing subordination. What it does mean is that two intelligent, spiritual, thoroughly equal people bring their resources together. They come to a mutual agreement, and the head makes sure that it happens. That's when families flourish.

The children are respectful

"Honor your father and mother that it may be well with you," the Bible says. "This is the first commandment with promise."

Someone may say, "My father was a drunk. He regularly beat my mother, and he abused me as a child. And you want me to respect him?" To such, my answer is: "No, I don't want you to respect his alcoholism. I don't want you to respect his brutality, and I don't want you to respect his sexual aberrations. I don't think that God does either. He detests those things. But what God does say is this: Accept the fact that, bad as he is, he is still your father. Respect him for that. Under God he was the means of your existing, and you should never forget that."

A daughter may say: "I never did get along with my mother. When I was a girl, we began to clash. It was about little things at first, but then she didn't approve of the guy that I married, and she wouldn't come to the wedding. Now she is always finding fault with the way I bring up her grandchildren. I never did get along with my mother." I don't think that God says a daughter has to get along with her mother. What God says is this: Recognize that for nine months you were inside her body; without her, you would not exist. She went through pain and brought you into the world. She was the means of caring for you in those early days. So respect her for that. Thank her for that, and respect her for being your mother. Try to see what she was doing when she raised you, and why things went the way they did.

The ideal home is where Father is acting as head, Mother adds her support, and the children are being brought up so that they don't have to be coerced into respecting their parents—there is an attitude of mutuality, love, and concern.

The family affirms itself

By this I mean that members of the family are committed to the family. Our society is currently full of fragmenting families. We used to operate on the basis of the extended family. Now we have become the "nuclear family." And the nuclear family is exploding, as nuclear things can. What we are finding is the total fragmentation of relationships.

When Jill and I moved from England to the United States, one of our major concerns was that we were taking our children away from their extended family; we were putting them down in a foreign land, where they had no grandparents. And that has been a concern of ours all the time we have lived in America.

There is something to be said for that ongoing, extended family, for that network of relationships, and for the wisdom and experience that extended family can provide. Building these relationships requires all family members to regard family life as a priority. Children must be interested in their parents. Parents must have time for their children. And siblings must be interested in each other. People must make family a priority.

The Lord adds his blessing

The final element that causes the family to flourish is that when all of this is happening, the Lord adds his blessing. By that I mean that he gives families the sense that he is at work in their lives individually and corporately and is bringing to pass his eternal purposes.

What kind of family stays together? The family in which family is important to the individuals in it. The family based on God's ideal and supported by prayer. Genuine families don't just happen; they require work from everyone involved. Unfortunately, too many people are giving up on their families—or they just don't care. We can never know the rich benefits of God's genuine family until we take hold of these relationships wholeheartedly, depending on the Holy Spirit's guidance as we all grow up together.

Let's Get Practical

1. Why are there no absolute guarantees for creating or maintaining a happy family life?

2. On what is a solid marriage founded?

3. Name some characteristics that often contribute to failure in a family. To which characteristics is your family the most vulnerable, and how can you work on making the situation better?

4. What are some key contributions to a family's stability made by Mom and Dad? By the children?

5. How will you work to strengthen the ties in your family?

10

Genuine Christians Are Distinctive in a Fallen World

Since the early days of the Christian church, controversy has raged over the proper way for Christians to behave and relate to the world. Hudson Taylor once said, "If your father and mother, your sister and brother—if the very cat and dog in the house—are not happier for your being a Christian, it is a question whether you really are."

The apostle Paul was quite clear in his assessment of how Christians should live. This is noted in two passages of Scripture:

I have written you in my letter not to associate with sexually immoral people—not at all meaning the people of this world who are immoral, or the greedy and swindlers, or idolaters. In that case you would have to leave this world. But now I am writing you that you must not associate with anyone who calls himself a brother but is sexually immoral or greedy, an idolater or a slanderer, a drunkard or a swindler. With such a man do not even eat.

What business is it of mine to judge those outside the church? Are you not to judge those inside? God will judge those outside. "Expel the wicked man from among you." (1 Cor. 5:9-13, NIV)

Do you not know that the wicked will not inherit the kingdom of God? Do not be deceived: Neither the sexually immoral nor idolaters nor adulterers nor male prostitutes nor homosexual offenders nor thieves nor the greedy nor drunkards nor slanderers nor swindlers will inherit the kingdom of God. And that is what some of you were. But you were washed, you were sanctified, you were justified in the name of the Lord Jesus Christ and by the Spirit of our God. (1 Cor. 6:9-11, NIV)

This is what I call straight talk. Paul doesn't mince words as he addresses some major problems in the church at Corinth. It is interesting that pollsters have observed two developments in the current American scene. First, there seems to be an increased interest and involvement in organized religion in America. Second, there is also evidence of a drastic collapse and disintegration in moral standards. Chuck Colson succinctly summarized these findings: "Religion is up, but morality is down."

This dichotomy has puzzled pollsters. With an increasing number of people claiming to have a vital relationship with God, one would expect them to live according to the teachings and in the power of the living Christ. The natural effect should be a more dramatic change in society than we are seeing. Why is this not happening? How is it possible that religion can be up and morality down? If the church is composed of people who are truly Christ's, shouldn't it have a greater impact on society and change its moral tone?

Apparently this is not happening. Some think that Christians are not practicing the moral implications of their faith. Is it possible to be a Christian and not be concerned with certain moral implications? Shouldn't our behavior be radically changed because of the belief to which we now adhere? We seem to be faced with a very serious situation.

Some years ago, when my wife and I visited Edinburgh, Scotland, we toured the magnificent castle that towers over the city. It had been built on a steep precipice overlooking a lake. The lake bed, now empty, is the site of railroad tracks that come into the center of the city. When the castle was built, it had a ready-made moat and was practically impregnable. In fact, the Edinburgh castle was captured only once in its long history, but not because of outside attack. A traitor on the inside opened the doors and let the enemy in.

Similarly, some people think that the major problem confronting our church and society is not external but internal. The enemy lies within in the sense that we have failed to apply the moral implications of our faith. Have Christians failed to link belief and behavior to form a distinctive lifestyle? In the rest of this chapter, we will deal with the necessity for Christians to integrate correct belief and behavior, the fundamentals of Christian experience, and our different standard of expectations for Christians as opposed to non-Christians.

The Integration of Belief and Behavior

Let's look at the connection between behavior and belief with Paul's words as a backdrop. As we have indicated, the apostle was addressing some serious problems in the church at Corinth, a city known for its morally reprobate behavior. In fact, they had coined a word for it in the Greek: To "Corinthianize" was to be involved in every kind of immoral behavior. The church in Corinth was made up of people who were just emerging from a corrupt and immoral society. Paul was telling them that a different kind of behavior was now expected of them as believers.

The apostle's sense of humor is evident in 1 Corinthians 5:10, where he says, "In that case you would have to leave this world." In his original letter he did not mean that the Corinthians were not to associate with immoral people. To do so, they would have had to leave the world, because immoral people were overrunning the place! Instead, he meant that they were not to associate with people who called themselves fellow Christians but continued in their immoral behavior. Simply put, we are to expect more from a believer, because there is a direct connection between morality and theology. If one's belief is real, it must affect one's behavior. Paul identifies three fundamentals of Christian belief.

Belief in the kingdom of God

Paul makes his point here by reminding the Corinthians that the wicked (their condition before Christ entered their lives) cannot inherit the kingdom of God. "Do you not know," he asks in 1 Corinthians 6:9, "that the wicked will not inherit the kingdom of God?" In 1 Corinthians 4:20 he had reminded them that "the kingdom is not a matter of talk but of power." It is a matter of dynamic living.

Paul's teaching about the kingdom of God can be summarized as follows: The kingdom of God consists of people who have surrendered their lives to God; everyone is not in it; the wicked will not be in it; and there are entrance requirements.

Some people are not interested in the kingdom of God or in submitting their lives to the lordship of Christ. They come under the rule of evil, or what the Scriptures call the kingdom of this world, ruled by Satan himself. The Bible makes it clear that each of us is part of one kingdom or the other.

Paul says that people who persist in evil will not inherit the kingdom of God. This means that they will not come under God's control either in this life or in eternity. Persons who live independently or antagonistically toward God in this world will find themselves separated from God in the world to come. However, it is possible to move from the kingdom of evil to the kingdom of God—if we change our allegiance.

How does a person enter the kingdom of God? Jesus answered this question when he was talking to Nicodemus: "Unless a man is born again, he cannot see the kingdom of God. . . . He cannot enter the kingdom of God." (John 3:3, 5, NIV)

To be born again or, more accurately, to be born from above, means that God has done a work of grace in my life. As a result, I have a tremendous desire to bring it joyfully and willingly under his control. I gladly submit myself to him for forgiveness, direction, power—indeed, for a whole new life. I am born again of the Spirit of God. I step out of darkness into light, as the Bible puts it, or out of death into life.

Some people can identify specifically the time of their conversion to Christ. Some have had dramatic, even traumatic, encounters with him. The apostle Paul's experience on the road to Damascus is a perfect example of this kind of conversion (see Acts 9). Paul undoubtedly remembered that event for the rest of his life.

If this were the only kind of conversion that counted, I, for one, would be left out. From my earliest days, I learned about God, Jesus, and salvation. In fact, I can honestly say that I can't recall a time when I wasn't aware of God's reality and presence. I cannot point to a clear-cut moment when I accepted Christ, but at some point in my childhood I did indeed step across the line to take my place with God's people. Without a doubt I know that I'm his child today.

Look at it this way. Do I know that I am physically alive only because I remember the minute details of my birth? No! But I'm definitely alive—with or without that memory. How do people know that they are born again? We know we are born again because of the newness of our lives.

Perhaps from your earliest days you knew of the Lord Jesus and in a very simple way responded to what you knew. You opened up like a flower to him. Or perhaps you resisted the Lord for years, but one day, like the apostle Paul, you were born again dramatically. The way you came to God is not that important. Of more importance is your acknowledgment that you did not want to live your life independently of God. Rather, you wanted to come under his benevolent, eternal control.

Belief in the Lord Jesus Christ

Another area we must deal with is our belief concerning the person of Christ. We return to 1 Corinthians 6:11, where Paul says, "That is what some of you were. But you were washed, you were sanctified, you were justified in the name of the Lord Jesus Christ and by the Spirit of our God."

The offices of Christ's full title, the Lord Jesus Christ, need to be acknowledged. The name Jesus means "Savior." When we call him Christ we are indicating that he was specially anointed by God to do what no one else could do. When we speak of him as Lord, we are recognizing that final authority resides in him. That is why we should be careful to recognize all aspects of Christ when we are referring to him. He is the Lord Jesus Christ.

What does all of this mean? It means that when I am confronted by the message of the Lord Jesus Christ, I have to decide whether I believe that he is the Savior of the world in general and that he is prepared to save me from my sins in particular. I need to decide whether he is the Christ, not one of many christs—whether he is one of many ways to come to the Father or the Way, the Anointed One of the Father. And if he is the Lord, will I make him the Lord of my life? Will I live in glad subjection to him, seeking to serve and honor him in all that I do?

Belief in the Holy Spirit

Again, we notice that the Corinthians came into the Christian experience "in the name of the Lord Jesus Christ and by the Spirit of our God." The Christian life cannot be separated from belief in the ministry of the Holy Spirit. In John 16, while giving some final instructions to his disciples, the Lord Jesus promised: "When he, the Spirit of truth, comes, he will guide you into all truth" (v. 13). The Holy Spirit, the third member of the Trinity, was sent by the Father after Christ returned to glory. In part, the ministry of the Holy Spirit would be to convict the world of sin, righteousness, and the judgment to come. We usually associate "conviction" with the courtroom, but it is also a good biblical word that means to convince deeply, to prick the conscience, to stir up a sense of guilt.

People sometimes say to me, "Don't lay a guilt trip on me." I reply, "I don't have to—God already did it by his Spirit. I don't need to stir it up." God, if he is working in our lives by his Spirit, is making us uncomfortable about the persons we are and what we have done. He is forcing us to confront the sin in our lives, and he is showing us what he desires for us. All of us recognize that ultimately we are accountable to God in the final judgment. That is the work of the Holy Spirit.

I have learned something after preaching for nearly forty years. Despite all of my skill and devotion in sermon preparation and delivery, what I say can roll off my listeners like water off a duck's back. Why? Unless the Spirit of God is taking the truth as it is proclaimed and winging it home to people's hearts, there is no impact at all. It is ultimately the Holy Spirit who ministers to the hearts of people. He makes the preaching and teaching of the Bible fit into their lives.

Let's put all of this together. Do you believe in the kingdom? Do you know what it is, how to get there, and who will be there and who won't? Do you know who the Lord Jesus is? Do you know about his lordship, his messiahship, his saviorhood? And do you know that the Holy Spirit really speaks to people, convicting them in order that he might convert them to Christ? This is fundamental belief. If we are going to talk about Christians getting their act together, we must make sure that these fundamental beliefs are in their lives.

Three Fundamentals of Christian Experience

This leads us to the fundamentals of Christian experience. The Corinthians had been washed, sanctified, and justified in the name of the Lord Jesus Christ and by the Spirit of God (1 Cor. 6:11). Christians who are truly in the kingdom have known these three experiences.

Christians were washed

What does the apostle say about the experience of being washed? He reminds the Corinthians of the moral corruption in their old lives and defines the actions that are unacceptable to God. He also reminds them that our words, our desires, and our actions reflect our moral corruption and failure, and that we cannot enter God's kingdom in this condition. "Do you not know that the wicked will not inherit the kingdom of God?" Paul asks (1 Cor. 6:9, NIV). How can we enter the kingdom of God when we have been living dirty lives? To do so, we need to be washed, purified, and forgiven. All of these terms describe the cleansing we so desperately need.

The Scriptures are full of references to this purifying or cleansing process. Some of these verses are found in hymns that are practically meaningless to many people today. The English poet and hymn writer William Cowper wrote:

There is a fountain filled with blood
Drawn from Emmanuel's veins
And sinners, plunged beneath that flood,
Lose all their guilty stains.

To a person unfamiliar with the cleansing power of Christ's blood, this verse seems grotesque. But to the Christian who has experienced the forgiveness provided by Christ's sacrifice on the cross, it is a beautiful expression. Whatever we have done, however wicked we have been, either in thought, word, or deed, God desires to forgive us. To be washed is an integral part of the Christian experience.

Christians are sanctified

The second fundamental of Christian experience is that of being sanctified. This word is also virtually unknown today. It refers to the word *saints*, used in all of the New Testament. "Do you not know that the saints will judge the world?" asks Paul (1 Cor. 6:2, NIV). These people have not been canonized; they are Corinthian believers who have been sanctified. A sanctified person is a saint; a saint is one who is sanctified. If you have been washed in the blood of Christ, you have been sanctified.

To be sanctified means that we are set apart and that we have a new status in life. Corinthians had lived sinful lives, but now they have been washed. They have come into a whole new position. They are new people—washed and sanctified.

The Bible describes sanctification in two ways. First, the moment I came to Christ I was washed and sanctified. Second, the process of sanctification continues for the rest of my life. I have been given a new status, but it takes the rest of my life to fulfill it.

Let me illustrate. As a young man, I was drafted into the Marines. Their magnificent dress uniform attracted me, and I thought that I would get one of those uniforms immediately. But they didn't give me one for months. When I asked about it, they told me, "You are a Marine. The moment you walked through the gates, you became a Marine. You are a Marine to stay." I said, "Give me another uniform then." They replied, "You are not fit to wear one yet. We will have to do something about your back, about your chest, and about your shoulders. We'll have to teach you how to march, how to walk, how to look like a Marine, and how to behave like a Marine. Then you can wear the uniform." I was a Marine the moment I was sworn into that position, but it took me a long, long time to wear the uniform.

I was sanctified the minute that I was washed. But it will take me the rest of my life to learn how to behave in a sanctified way.

Christians are justified

The third fundamental of the Christian experience is justification. This word is of particular interest to lawyers and accountants. Imagine that you have appeared in court before God, who has charged you with living a wicked, sinful life. You are found guilty as charged. God says that anyone guilty of such behavior cannot inherit the kingdom of God. But at that moment, the Lord Jesus stands up in court as your advocate. "Father, one moment please," he says. "I agree that everything you said is true, but please remember that I have actually accepted the total penalty for this sin. Therefore, because this person has already been judged in me and I have accepted full payment for these misdeeds, I ask you to please release the prisoner at the bar."

God replies, "Certainly." He looks down at you and says, "There is no further charge against you. You are thoroughly forgiven. You may go." That is one aspect of justification. The justified person revels in Paul's words to the Romans: "Therefore, there is no condemnation for those who are in Christ Jesus" (8:1, NIV).

Accountants like the idea of justification for another reason. They like it because God keeps the books in heaven. In his master book, he has a record of all our wrongdoings. But when we come to Christ and are washed and sanctified, God adds up all that we have done and credits it to Christ. Then he adds up all that Christ has done and credits it to us. We are left standing on the righteousness of Christ. We've been justified.

Let me ask you. Do you have your beliefs straight about the kingdom of God, and the Lord, and the Spirit? Has your experience been brought into line to some degree? Do you know that you have been washed, justified, and sanctified?

A Holy People

Be imitators of God, therefore, as dearly loved children and live a life of love, just as Christ loved us and gave himself up for us as a fragrant offering and sacrifice to God.

But among you there must not be even a hint of sexual immorality, or of any kind of impurity, or of greed, because these are improper for God's holy people. (Eph. 5:1-3, NIV)

The word *holy* makes many people uncomfortable, but it simply means to be distinctive, to be different. God uses it to describe himself as well as his people. We are to be different; we are to be distinct.

Scripture tells us that a distinct, holy lifestyle is the result of living in love, as stated in the Ephesians quote above. For husbands, this is reinforced by verse 25: "Husbands, love your wives." If husbands honestly love their wives as the Scriptures instruct, they will definitely stand out in any society.

Why should this emphasis on love appeal, not only to husbands, but to all believers? First, as Paul tells us, we are dearly loved children. We understand the love of God for us and have some insight into what love really means. This becomes the stimulus for a loving relationship in every area of our lives. Distinctive Christians will be holy because of their own experience of the love of God.

Another factor prompting our love is that Christ loved us and gave himself up for us. The only reason we have peace with God is that our sins have been forgiven through Christ's love. We have been redeemed by his sacrificial love. Without the love of God and Christ, we are nothing. Believers who recognize this begin to practice love. If we are unsure about how to love others, further, specific principles are laid out for us in 1 Corinthians 13.

We live as holy people when we live in the light: "For you were once darkness, but now you are light in the Lord. Live as children of light" (Eph. 5:8, NIV). Living out of touch with God is like living in darkness, where evil and confusion reign. But when we come to know Christ, we are introduced to the light and get a new perspective on life. Because we can see with new eyes and new hearts, we are able to live in new ways.

Living in the light requires three separate actions. First, we must reject the darkness. Next, we need to reflect the fruit of light, which Paul describes in verse 9: "The light consists in all goodness, righteousness and truth." When we live in the light of the knowledge of God through our Lord Jesus Christ, we become interested in what is good and right and true.

Third, we must respect the Lord's wishes as indicated in verse 10: "Find out what pleases the Lord." Many people are only interested in pleasing themselves and expect everyone else to please them, too. Some are dedicated to pleasing their spouse, above and beyond any other guiding principle. While it is important to be attentive to the wants and needs of our husband or wife, we must remember that he or she is human and fallible, after all, and it is not wise to make his or her voice the final authority on our lives.

Others become enslaved to pleasing other people (one current term for this is "codependence"), and their lives become fragmented by the many different demands made upon them by others. But there is something infinitely more important here than pleasing yourself, or pleasing your spouse, or pleasing your peers: It is pleasing the Lord.

We live as holy people before God when we submit to one another because we are all one in Christ. The Living Bible paraphrases Ephesians 5:21-22:

> Honor Christ by submitting to each other. You wives must submit to your husbands' leadership in the same way you submit to the Lord.

This idea of wives submitting to their husbands as to the Lord is wrapped up in the idea of all believers submitting to one another. Thus, to live in the Lord, we must submit to him and to each other.

What enables us to be submissive in the midst of a culture that scorns submission and screams about taking care of Number One? "Do not get drunk on wine. . . . Instead, be filled with the Spirit" (Eph. 5:18). When we live in the fullness of the Spirit, we generate a submissive attitude toward other Christians. When we live in the fullness of the Spirit, we have no need to puff ourselves up, as is so common in our society. We can be confident, calm, giving, and loving, because we are

> a chosen people, a royal priesthood, a holy nation, a people belonging to God that you may declare the praises of him who called you out of darkness into his wonderful light. Once you were not a people, but now you are the people of God; once you had not received mercy, but now you have received mercy. Dear friends, I urge you, as aliens and strangers in the world, to abstain from sinful desires, which war against your soul. Live such good lives among the pagans that, though they accuse you of doing wrong, they may see your good deeds and glorify God on the day he visits us. (1 Pet. 2:9-12)

The Double Standard of Expectations

We began this chapter by pointing out that belief should affect behavior; and we said if it doesn't, we may legitimately question a person's relationship to the Lord. In fact, the apostle Paul calls for a double standard in our attitudes toward the people around us. We are to expect more from believers than from unbelievers. Believers are to follow a different and distinctive lifestyle, translating their theology into morality. People who have been washed should not jump right back into the pigpen. Those who have been justified should not want their accounts reopened. Those who have been sanctified should be willing to be set apart for God's service.

That is why the church must exercise discipline. Indeed, we Christians have an obligation to discipline those who identify themselves with believers, yet fall back into the wicked ways of the world. The Bible tells us to say to them, "I'm sorry, but unless you recognize the error of your ways, we can have nothing to do with you." In so doing, we are not sitting in judgment upon them; we are trying to bring them to repentance.

Let me bring this closer to home. How should Christians react to those who are at the heart of a scandalous, immoral situation? Until the people involved honestly repent of their excesses and of their wrongdoing, we must refuse to have fellowship with them or welcome them into our churches. They have failed to make the connection between belief and behavior.

There are biblical models to follow with regard to our treatment of unbelievers who are caught in the web of sin. Jesus gave us a perfect example in his dealing with the woman caught in adultery. First he told her accusers, "If any one of you is without sin, let him be the first to throw a stone at her" (John 8:7, NIV). Then, after she told him that no one had cast a stone, he went on, "then neither do I condemn you. . . . Go now and leave your life of sin" (vv. 10-11). He did not excuse her sin. Instead, he expected her lifestyle to demonstrate the higher morality of the Christian walk. If we want to convey our beliefs to people, we will gain credibility by living morally before them.

What happens when Christians (or people who call themselves Christians) get confused at this point? First, there is the confusion of mistaken belief. Paul deals with this problem in 1 Corinthians 6:9-11, where he clearly indicates that the wicked will not inherit the kingdom of God; and then he identifies the wicked. In spite of this clear communication, we tend to be deceived about this today. Many have the idea that "everything will come out in the wash. Everybody is going to be in heaven in the end, so it really doesn't make much difference how we live." Clearly, this is not what the Bible teaches.

Some people are confused by society's new terminology for behavior that the Bible has always called sin. On the one hand, Paul speaks of sexual immorality, adultery, male prostitutes, homosexual offenders, and drunkards. On the other hand, society uses terms and phrases like "experiencing the sexual revolution," "meaningful relationships outside unhappy marriages," "another sexual preference," and "people with alcohol dependency." I am not suggesting that these new terms have no significance. I am saying, however, that society's polite euphemisms can be very confusing at times, because they remove the stigma of sin from many illicit activities.

David once prayed, "Keep your servant also from willful sins; may they not rule over me. Then will I be blameless, innocent of great transgression" (Ps. 19:13, NIV).

The King James Version translates this verse: "Keep back thy servant also from presumptuous sins." Paul is condemning this attitude in his letter to the Corinthians. People who are guilty of this kind of sin will not inherit the kingdom of God. We must not be confused into thinking that once we have been redeemed, it really doesn't matter how we live. On the contrary, it matters very much.

There is also some confusion about false profession. In 1 Corinthians 5:9-11 Paul counsels us to avoid anyone who claims to be a brother, but who also continues to be sexually immoral, a drunkard, a swindler, and the like. Such a person is calling himself a brother, but in all probability, he is not a real Christian at all.

A word of clarification is in order here. The Bible is not teaching that once you are washed, sanctified, and justified, you are perfect. It doesn't say that an individual Christian is incapable of falling back into old, well-used patterns. It is saying that if you come across someone who claims to be a believer but persists in an unbecoming lifestyle, that person should not be believed. You should put some distance between that person and yourself.

We are not talking about perfection; nor are we just talking about the possibility of slipping. *We are talking about that ongoing commitment to a lifestyle that is the direct antithesis of all that is meant by being washed, sanctified, and justified.*

In the fall of the year, the oak trees in my backyard start to lose their leaves, and over the course of several weeks most of those leaves end up on the ground. But have you noticed that there are always some isolated leaves left on the branches? Some fussy people I know get on a ladder to knock those last leaves down.

I have a better idea for them; just leave them where they are, and in the spring they will come fluttering down. Why? Because the sap will start to flow, and when it does, new life begins to come, and it pushes off the old leaves.

Do you know what happens with the people who have been washed, sanctified, and justified? We don't need to pluck off the leaves of their old life. We just teach them and love them, exercising patience and compassion. We wait for the sap to begin to flow. And when it does, the new spiritual life begins to come, and the old leaves drop off.

To complete the analogy, we should be concerned about the person who says that "the sap is flowing," but the old leaves don't fall off. Then you have a problem. Jesus put it this way:

Watch out for false prophets. They come to you in sheep's clothing, but inwardly they are ferocious wolves. By their fruit you will recognize them. . . . Every good tree bears good fruit, but a bad tree bears bad fruit. A good tree cannot bear bad fruit, and a bad tree cannot bear good fruit. Every tree that does not bear good fruit is cut down and thrown into the fire. Thus, by their fruit you will recognize them. (Matt. 7:15-20, NIV)

How do we confirm our belief? By our behavior. Belief unrelated to behavior is not the norm for spiritual experience. When we get our theology straight, our morality will demonstrate that belief eventually. However, morality doesn't automatically point to correct theology. It's not a case of either/or. I cannot say, "I am a very moral person; therefore, I don't need the Lord Jesus Christ and the Spirit of God. I am a very good person; therefore, I don't need to be washed, justified, and sanctified." (It's important to remember that people can behave well outwardly but remain unchanged in their basic attitudes.) Belief and behavior travel in tandem. True belief and true experience result in a newness of lifestyle. Newness of life comes because we understand the dynamics needed to live in the power of the Holy Spirit.

I am sure that I'm addressing two kinds of readers. Some can honestly say that they are living before the Lord with a deep desire to bring belief and behavior into line with one another. They are translating what they are into what they do.

On the other hand, some must confess, "I'm just pretending. If others could see through the polite, 'churchy' facade I hide behind, they would be appalled." To you I would say, "Surrender your life to the power of the Holy Spirit. Let him work his miracle in your life."

Please remember, the Lord doesn't expect us to be perfect. He's looking for a positive growth curve, progression "toward the goal to win the prize for which God has called [us] heavenward in Christ Jesus," says Paul in Philippians 3:14. Real Christians are distinctive people, standing out with God's brilliance in our dark world.

Let's Get Practical

1. Explain these three basic Christian beliefs.

   belief in the kingdom of God:

   belief in the Lord Jesus Christ:

   belief in the Holy Spirit:

2. How do these beliefs effect our behavior?

3. What do these three fundamentals of the Christian life mean, and how have you experienced them?

   we are washed:

   we are sanctified:

   we are justified:

4. Why are we to be holy? How can human beings be holy?

5. How has being a believer in Jesus made you distinctive in a world that does not know him? In which areas are you not yet distinctive, and how might you allow God to work in these areas?